Until Death do us Part

Story: Hiroshi Takashige
Art: DOUBLE-S

Until Death do us Part

Until Death do us Part

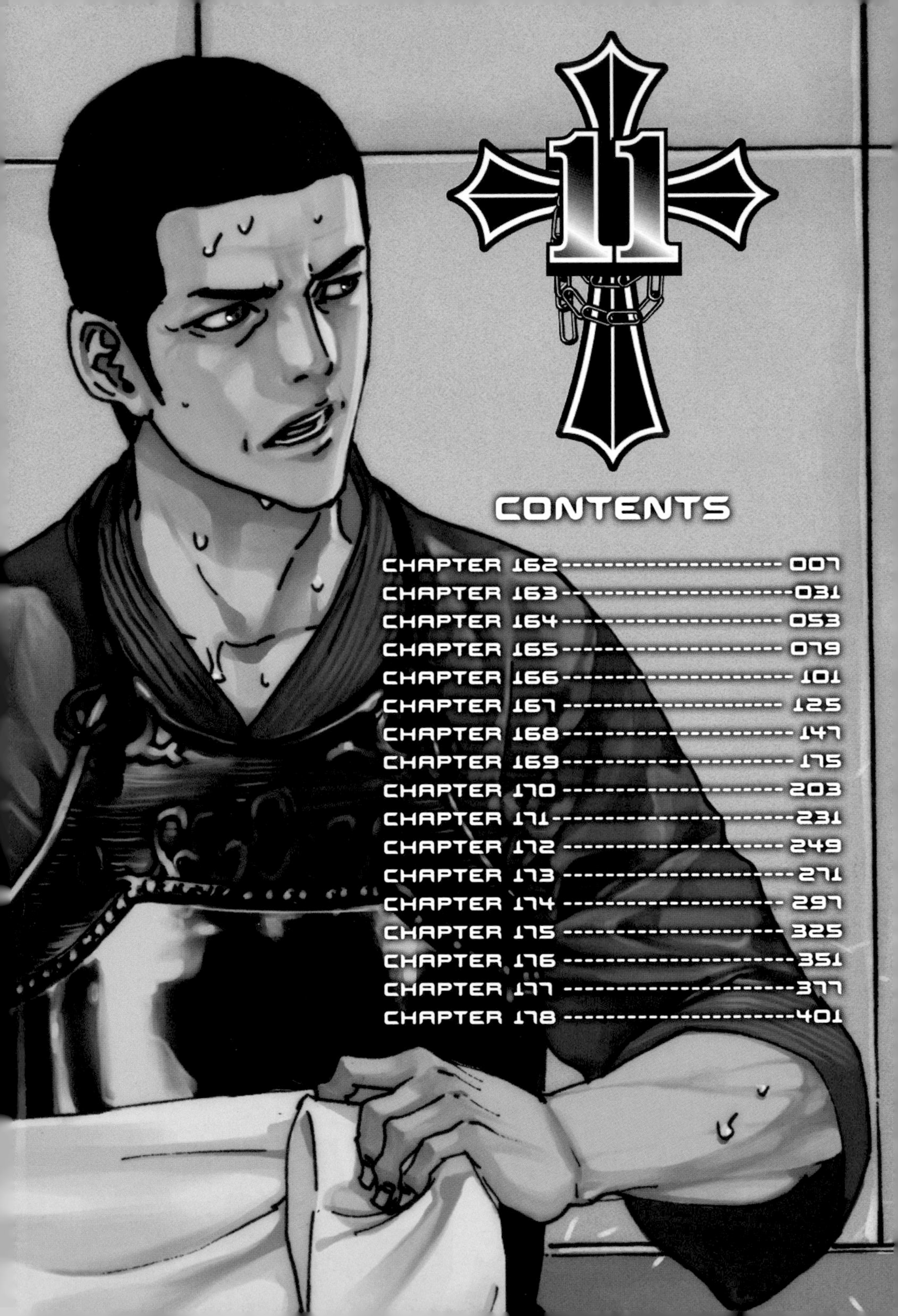

11

CONTENTS

ONE OF THE KEYS TO MASTERING AN ULTIMATE SWORD SWING IS THE SPEED OF THE BLADE.

THE SWORD IS SPEED!
THIS WILL SETTLE IT!!!

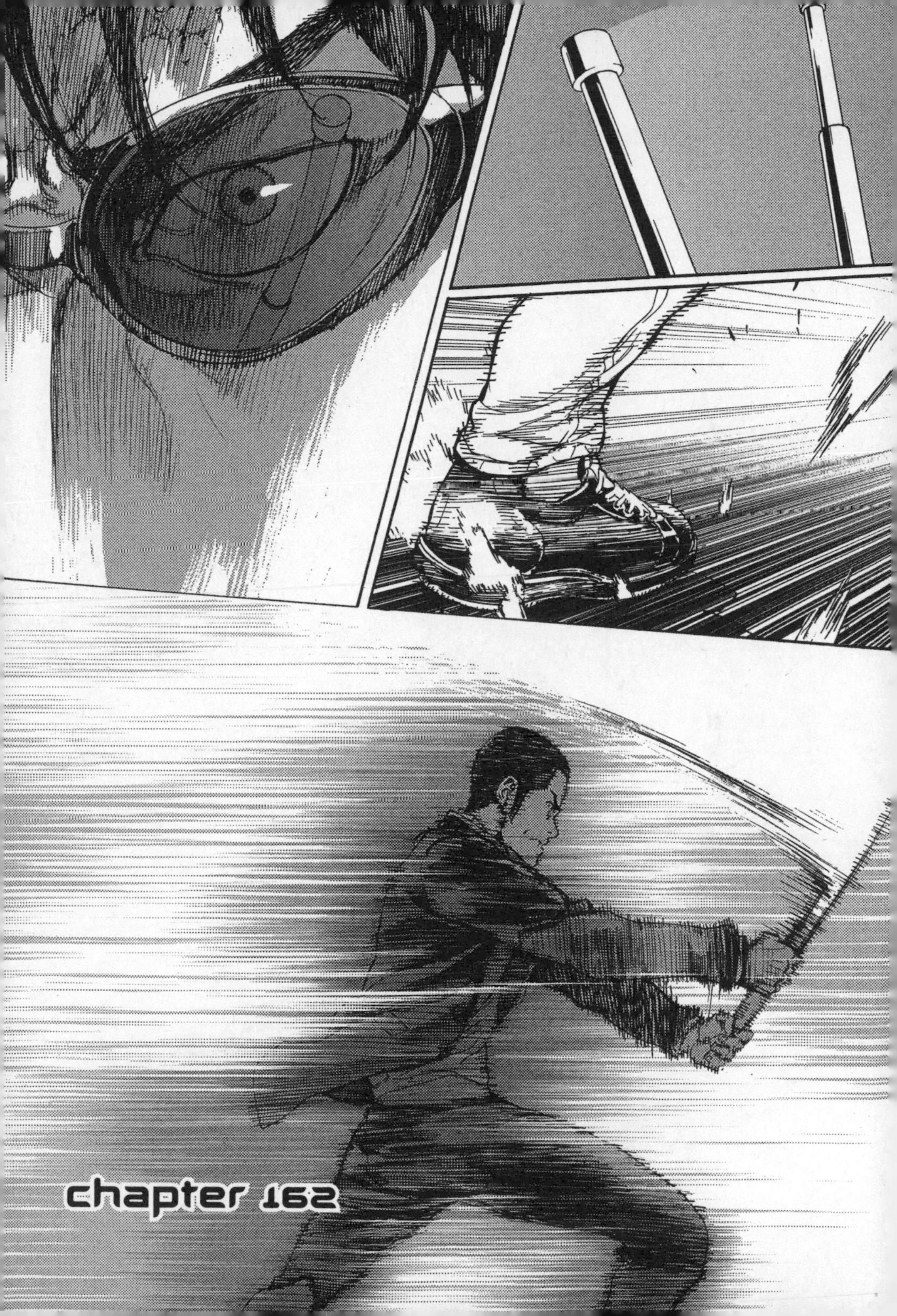
chapter 162

キンッ
KIN
(TING)
ZUSHAAA
(ZSHHK)

...

HOW CAN THIS BE...!?

スウ…
SUU (SHH)
I'VE LOST...
KACHI (CLICK)
...

NO, YOU HAVEN'T.
THAT WAS SIMPLY THE DIFFERENCE BETWEEN KATANA AND POLICE BATON.

...LIAR...
HE CAUGHT THE TIP OF MY BATON PERFECTLY.

NORMALLY ONE STRIKES DOWN AT THE TIP OF THE OPPONENT'S DESCENDING SWORD.
THIS INTERSECTION IS THE ULTIMATE COMBINATION—AN ATTACKING SWING THAT SUCCEEDS AT DEFENDING AS WELL.
BY STRIKING IT AND DEFLECTING ITS PATH, YOU DEFEND AGAINST THE ENEMY'S ATTACK DURING YOUR SWING.

A TECHNIQUE FROM THE SINGLE-BLADED MAKABE SCHOOL.
SINCE IT'S MEANT TO CHIP AWAY AT THE ENEMY'S SWING...

...IT'S KNOWN AS THE "BLADE-CHIPPER."
AND THIS IS WHAT'S POSSIBLE WHEN THAT SKILL IS MASTERED...

!?
バラ
BARA (CRUMBLE)

THAT WAS QUITE A SHOW YOU PUT ON.

IT WAS ONLY POSSIBLE AGAINST A SKILLED OPPONENT WHOSE BLADE WOULDN'T WAVER.
LIKE WE AGREED, I'M TAKING EBATA WITH ME.

I HAVE NO MEANS TO STOP YOU ANYMORE, ANYWAY.
DO AS YOU WILL.

HOWEVER! IF YOU ACT IRRESPONSIBLY TOWARD ANY OTHER CIVILIANS...
...I WILL RISK MY LIFE TO STOP YOU.

YOU HAVE MY WORD.

SEVERAL DAYS LATER—

DOGAAN (KABLAMM)

WILL THAT DO THE JOB?
WHO THE HELL DO YOU THINK YOU'RE TALKING TO?

I DON'T KNOW. I ONLY KNOW YOU'RE SUPPOSED TO BE AN EXPLOSIVES EXPERT.

LOCATION, EXPLOSION, AND SET-UP.
I MADE SURE NONE OF THESE HARMED ANYONE.

THEY DISCOVERED A DANGEROUS STRUCTURAL FLAW IN THAT BUILDING, AND THE COMPANY WAS DEBATING WHETHER TO SELL IT OFF OR DISMANTLE IT THEMSELVES.
TEARING IT DOWN GIVES THEM A PERFECTLY GOOD REASON TO REBUILD. NOW EVERY-ONE'S HAPPY.

WHY ARE YOU ACTING THIS WAY THOUGH?
YOU WOULDN'T FEEL ANY REMORSE ABOUT CUTTING THAT SCUMBAG IN TWO.

PRETTY EXTREME OPINION FOR SOME-ONE IN THE ORGANIZA-TION.

THAT'S BECAUSE I'M NOT IN THE NETWORK.
I'M A FREELANCE DEMOLITION MAN. SOME FOLKS KNOW ME BY THE HANDLE "PYRO."
YOUR BOSS SAVED MY ASS WHEN A PREVIOUS CLIENT WAS PREPARED TO KILL ME AFTER OUR BUSINESS PARTNER STABBED US IN THE BACK.

YOU SEEM PRETTY HONORABLE, FOR A CRIMINAL.

THE INJURY TO THE BOSS'S LEG WAS MY FAULT. I'LL STICK AROUND UNTIL HE'S BETTER.
BUT I DON'T MIND DOIN' THE WORK HERE, AS LONG AS IT'S HELPING PEOPLE.

WHAT ABOUT EBATA?

OUR STORY IS THAT HE "PASSED OUT ON A LOWER FLOOR."
WHILE TRYING TO FLEE THE BUILDING, THE EXPLOSION "HAPPENED EARLIER THAN HE PLANNED."

AND HOW WILL THE POLICE KNOW THAT?

I INTENTIONALLY PUT IN A PART THAT USES A DIFFERENT WAVELENGTH...
...WHICH CAUSED THE DIGITAL TIMER TO COUNT DOWN EARLIER THAN IT SHOULD HAVE.
THE REST IS A SIMPLE ENOUGH BOMB THAT EVEN AN AMATEUR LIKE HIM COULD PUT IT TOGETHER.

I SEE... A REAL PRO JOB, MOCKED UP TO LOOK CRUDE.

THIS'LL PUT HIM UP THE CREEK FOR ANOTHER TWENTY OR THIRTY YEARS.

BY THE TIME HE BREATHES FRESH AIR AGAIN, HE'LL BE LIKE TAROU URASHIMA, WELL INTO HIS FIFTIES.
IF HE ACTUALLY GETS OUT ON GOOD BEHAVIOR BEFORE THEN, I'LL JUST GO AFTER HIM AGAIN.
THAT'S A LOT OF WORK TO FRAME A GUY...

LIKE I CARE. THINK OF WHAT HE DID— HE STILL DESERVES WORSE.

I DON'T LIKE YOU MUCH, BUT I TOOK THIS ON BECAUSE THE GIRL ASKED ME TO. SO TAKE THIS WARNING TO HEART.
YOU'RE GOING WAY OVERBOARD ON THIS ONE.

YOU'D BETTER EXPECT THE NETWORK TO COME DOWN ON YOU.

I'M READY FOR IT.
...

POLICE HQ
SIGN: INTERROGATION ROOM
取調室
...
...
...!

BAG: EVIDENCE

WE'VE GOT PRINTS ON THE EXPLOSIVES AT THE SCENE, SO BASED ON EVIDENCE ALONE...
...WE CAN MAKE A PRETTY AIRTIGHT CASE.
HE'S GOT PRIORS, AND WHO KNOWS WHAT OTHER STUFF HE COULD HAVE GOTTEN UP TO THAT WE JUST DON'T KNOW ABOUT?
ON THIS CASE ALONE, WE CAN SLAP HIM WITH TERRORISM, BOMBING, DESTRUCTION OF PROPERTY, ASSAULT, ATTEMPTED MURDER...

A MOUNTAIN OF CHARGES WITH NOT A SINGLE FACTOR IN HIS FAVOR.
IF WE TURN UP ANYTHING ELSE DURING THE INVESTI-GATION...

...HE COULD BE LOOKING AT DEATH ROW...
YOU REAP WHAT YOU SOW.
PROBABLY WON'T FIND A BETTER SAYING TO SUM UP THIS ONE.

HEH HEH..
BWA HA HA...
GA HA HA HA HA HA HA HA HA!!
COME ON, GENDA-SAN.
THAT'S NOT RIGHT...
HA HA HA HA HA HA HA!!

SHUT UP AND LET ME LAUGH.
HAVE YOU EVER SEEN A MORE PICTURE-PERFECT EXAMPLE OF "REAPING WHAT YOU SOW"!?

IT'S OUR JOB TO ENSURE THAT CRIMINALS GET CHARGED WITH THE CRIMES THEY COMMITTED AND SERVE THEIR SENTENCES.
THIS IS THE PERFECT PUNISHMENT FOR A DESPICABLE, COWARDLY SLIMEBALL WHO ONLY TARGETED THOSE WEAKER THAN HIMSELF.
IF HE HAD TO BE CLEVERLY FRAMED FOR IT, THEN SO BE IT, HIJIKATA.

!?
WOULD SUCH A CRAFTY, CLEVER MAN REALLY INTENTIONALLY KILL MASTER?

SOMETHING WRONG?

NO. NOTHING.

GUESS I'LL REOPEN THAT CASE FOR MYSELF AND EXPOSE HIS TRUE NATURE...

GU
(BLUB)
グッ
GU
グッ
JUUU
(FZZZ)
ジュウウウ
PASHI
(THAK)
パシッ
BUN
(WHOOSH)

I ONLY DID IT BECAUSE THAT'S WHAT IGAWA TOLD ME TO DO.
...I WOULDN'T HAVE MINDED DRAGGING HIM THROUGH THE ENTIRE CITY AND FINISHING UP WITH A PUBLIC CRUCIFIXION.
IN FACT, I THINK IT'S ABOUT TIME THEY PUT THAT ONE BACK ON THE TABLE.

...LIKE A MAN OUT OF TIME...

FOOD'S NEARLY DONE. CALL IGAWA DOWN HERE.
SURE THING.

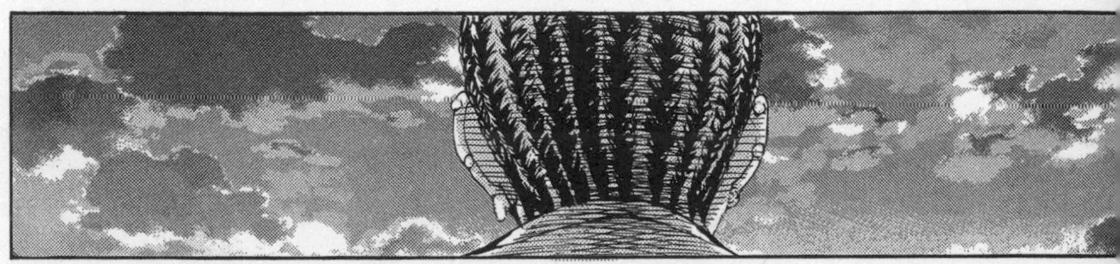

MAYBE I WAS WRONG.
MAYBE I'D FEEL BETTER IF I'D KILLED HIM, LIKE MAMORU SAID.
WOULD MAHO...
...FORGIVE ME FOR LETTING IT END LIKE THIS?

WHEN WE WERE CHASING HIM DOWN, I COULD TELL YOU WERE CONFLICTED.

I KEPT SEEING FUTURES WHERE THE CULPRIT WAS DEAD OR ALIVE, BACK AND FORTH.
IT WAS LIKE ANY LITTLE THING COULD HAVE DECIDED HIS FATE.

BUT THE ONLY TRULY PERMANENT DECISION WOULD BE KILLING HIM.
AND IF YOU REALLY DO END UP FEELING LIKE THIS WAS THE WRONG CHOICE, YOU HAVE THE OPTION OF CLEARING UP THE FALSE CHARGES.

I DON'T THINK I'LL EVER WANT TO DO THAT...
...BUT I SUPPOSE YOU'RE RIGHT.

NOT EVEN MAMORU-SAN OR THE PEOPLE IN THE NETWORK KNOW WHAT THE REAL "RIGHT ANSWER" IS.

FUTURES WHERE THE CULPRIT WAS ALIVE OR DEAD...
...AND I WAS RESPONSIBLE FOR HARUKA HAVING TO SEE THOSE AWFUL SCENES...
...

...
LET'S EAT DINNER, THEN.
SURE ...
カチャ
GACHA (CLICK)
キキィ
KIKII (SCREECH)

HERE YOU ARE, SIR.
GOOD.
BATAN (THUMP)
...LITTLE MISS... I'M TAKIN' CARE OF THIS OLD FELLA ON YOUR BODY-GUARD'S BEHALF.
ONLY BECAUSE HE TOLD ME THIS WAS FOR YOUR SAKE.

AND WHAT'S YOUR PLAN?
FOR NOW, PRO-CURING TALENT.
WE'LL NEED MANY DIFFERENT TALENTS ON THE GROUND.
POLICE HQ
GENDA-SAN.
YEAH?

WE'VE GOT A REQUEST FROM A JOURNALIST ASKING FOR YOU BY NAME.

JOUR-NALIST?
IT'S THROUGH SOME KIND OF KENDO THING—

FOR ME!?

WELL, YOU WERE THE PERENNIAL CHAMPIONSHIP CANDIDATE, RIGHT? IT SHOULDN'T BE THAT STRANGE ...

DON'T BE STUPID. THAT MIGHT BE THE STORY WITHIN THE DEPART-MENT...
...BUT I'VE NEVER ACTUALLY BEEN IN A TOURNAMENT. WHY WOULD A PUBLIC SOURCE COME TALK TO ME!?

SAID THEY WANTED TO SPEAK ABOUT THE "*BLADE DEMON.*"

…

I'M FREE AT THREE O'CLOCK TODAY.
WE'LL MEET OUTSIDE, SO GET A NAME AND LOCATION FROM THEM.
UH, OKAY.

STRANGE THAT HE'D ACCEPT…

IT'LL BE AT A CAFÉ IN YUURAKU-CHO. THE WRITER'S NAME IS TOORU MIZUSAWA.

TOORU MIZUSAWA? I'VE HEARD THAT NAME BEFORE …

IT CAN'T BE…

NOT THE POLICE, NOT A CRIMINAL, SOME-THING LESS OBVIOUS.
BUT... WHERE? HMMM...

THAT'S IT!

...HE'S THAT SPORTS-WRITER...
A REAL MUCKRAKER TYPE, DIGGING UP ALL KINDS OF SCANDALOUS DIRT ON THE FIGHTING WORLD.
DAMN... NOW I WISH I HADN'T SAID YES.

...

...
...

AHH, ENOUGH OF THIS!!
FORGET IT!!

I CAN'T FOCUS ON WORK UNTIL I CLEAR THIS UP.

...

FIGURES THAT SNEAKY LITTLE RAT WANTS SOME PRIVATE DIRT ON HIJIKATA'S MURDER OF OUR TEACHER SO HE CAN TURN IT INTO A BIG SCANDAL.

THAT'S PER-FECT.
I'LL BE ABLE TO DRAIN HIM OF EXACTLY THE INFOR-MATION I NEED.

GENDA-SAN, I PRESUME?
!?
MIZUSAWA.
AND... YOU ARE ...???

...A WOMAN?
IT'S A PEN NAME.
READERS FIND IT HARDER TO TRUST AN ARTICLE WITH A WOMAN'S NAME ON THE BYLINE.
...THAT LITTLE PRICK FAILED TO MENTION THE MOST CRUCIAL PART...

IT'S A STEREO-TYPE.
PEOPLE ASSUME THAT A WOMAN CANNOT POSSIBLY BE AS WELL VERSED IN SPORTS OR MARTIAL ARTS.

IT SEEMS YOU ALREADY UNDERSTAND WHAT I WANT, DON'T YOU?

...

HOKKAIDO

TSU
(PAUSE)
BUN
(WHOOSH)

GA
GA
GA
(WHAM)
GA
HYU
(SWISH)

BA (ZWIP)
GUI (TUG)
PASHI (SNAK)

NOT BAD...
THANK YOU, SIR.

I BET THAT WRITER'S GONE TO GENDA, JUST LIKE I TOLD HER TO.

HEH HEH.
BUT I GOT A REAL GOOD STORY OUT OF IT.

I'LL HAVE TO GO AND SHARE IT WITH HIM LATER.
...

IT'S NONE OF MY CONCERN.
IT'S MAMORU HIJIKATA WHOM I WANT TO COVER.
...

I'M RESEARCHING THE TRUTH BEHIND THE PRODIGY OF THE ANCIENT SWORD STYLE.
...

chapter 164

スッ
SU (SHFF)

WHAT DO YOU MEAN, COVER HIJIKATA?

I WOULD LIKE TO TURN HIS STORY INTO A NONFICTION BOOK.

IS IT... WORTHY OF A BOOK?

BASED ON MARKETABILITY, IT COULD BE, OR PERHAPS NOT. BUT I WANT TO WRITE ABOUT IT ANYWAY.
A GOOD PRODUCT IS ALWAYS WORTH THE TROUBLE.

...WHAT MADE YOU WANT TO WRITE ABOUT HIM?

IS SHE SERIOUS? I DON'T SENSE AN ULTERIOR MOTIVE...

HE'S ONE OF THOSE SWORD MASTERS WHOSE NAME IS ONLY KNOWN IN RARIFIED CIRCLES.
NOT TO BRAG OR ANYTHING, BUT EVEN I'M BETTER KNOWN IN THE COMBAT WORLD THAN HE IS.

YES... AT FIRST IT WAS JUST A PAGE-THREE INTEREST PIECE ABOUT A "DISCIPLE KILLING HIS MASTER."

I'M ASHAMED TO SAY THAT I HAVE TO RESORT TO WRITING SUCH ARTICLES IN ORDER TO MAKE A LIVING.
BUT I'VE NEVER MADE UP A STORY JUST TO SELL COPIES

I'VE SEEN YOUR WORK.
JUST NEVER READ IT— NOT MY TASTE.

BUT THE MORE I LOOKED INTO IT, THE MORE FASCINATING I FOUND HIM AS A PERSON.
WHAT ABOUT HIM DREW YOUR EYE?

LET'S SEE.... IF I HAD TO PUT IT INTO WORDS...

...HE SEEMS LIKE A MAN "BORN OUT OF TIME."

HMM...

BASED ON THE TESTIMONY I'VE COLLECTED FROM MY SOURCES SO FAR, IT'S QUITE EASY TO SUM UP HIS PERSONAL AMBITION.
HIS GOAL IS TO MASTER THE SWORD.

BUT WHAT MEANING DOES THAT HOLD IN MODERN SOCIETY?
...GOOD QUESTION ...

MAMORU HIJIKATA...

...POSSESSES A SENSE OF INTRANSIGENCE AS HE STRUGGLES WITH MODERN SOCIETY, AND THE TOUGHNESS OF SPIRIT TO CONTINUE ALONG HIS PATH.
IT'S A FIXATION ON MARTIAL WAYS THAT TRANSCENDS THE BOUNDARY OF MERE SPORT.
CAN YOU IMAGINE A MORE FASCINATING INDIVIDUAL?
...I SEE...
TO AN OUTSIDER, I'M SURE HE MUST SEEM VERY INTRIGUING.
IN THE FIVE YEARS SINCE HE VANISHED FROM CENTER STAGE, HE'S WANDERED AROUND TO SCHOOLS OF THE OLD WAYS...
AND FINALLY, THE SENSEI FROM THE KASHIMASHIN SCHOOL TOLD ME THAT YOU WERE LIKELY THE LAST TO SEE HIM.

...THE OLD BLABBER-MOUTH...

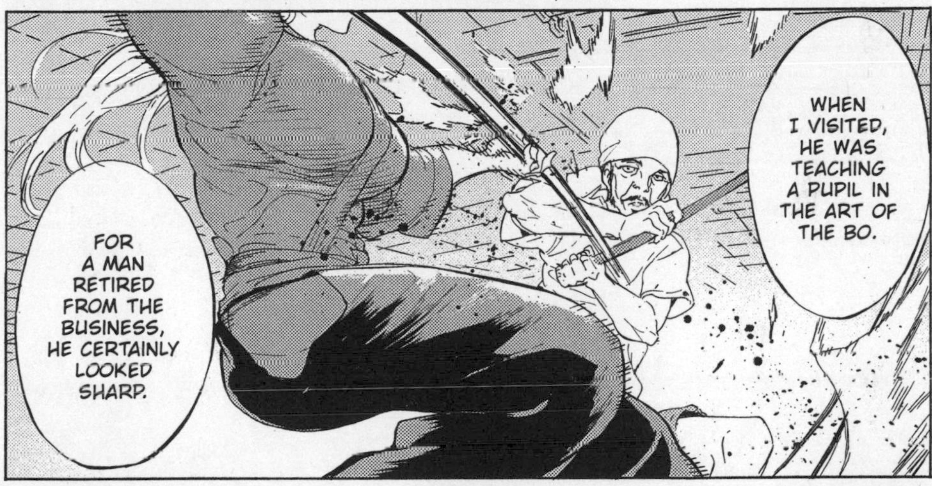
WHEN I VISITED, HE WAS TEACHING A PUPIL IN THE ART OF THE BO.
FOR A MAN RETIRED FROM THE BUSINESS, HE CERTAINLY LOOKED SHARP.

THE KASHIMASHIN STYLE IS A COMPOSITE STYLE WITH MANY FACETS. HE'S EVEN TOUGH BARE-HANDED.

UM... WHAT IS IT?

I DON'T HAVE THE TIME TO GO INTO DETAIL OR READ THIS OVER.
DO YOU MIND IF WE MEET AGAIN AFTER WORK HOURS?

OF COURSE. I'M SORRY TO KEEP YOU LIKE THIS.

HERE'S WHERE WE SHOULD MEET...

ABOUT TWENTY YEARS EARLIER—

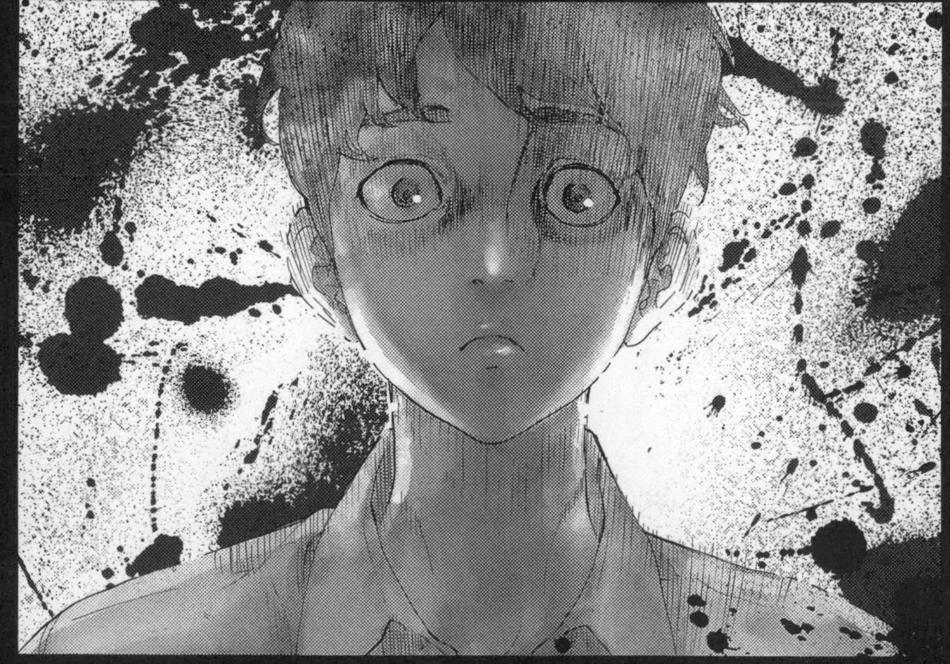

MAMORU LOST HIS PARENTS TO AN ACCIDENT CAUSED BY A DRUNK DRIVER.
HE WAS SENT TO LIVE WITH KATSUNOSHIN HIJIKATA, HIS PATERNAL GRANDFATHER AND ONLY LIVING RELATIVE.
AS A LONGTIME PRACTITIONER OF THE JIKISHINKAGE STYLE, HE WAS A DISCIPLINED MAN.

THIS WAS MAMORU HIJIKATA'S FIRST BRUSH WITH THE ANCIENT WAYS.

ONCE HE SHOWED INTEREST IN THE SWORD, MAMORU'S GRAND-FATHER WAS INITIALLY HIS DIRECT TEACHER.
BUT THE BOY LEARNED SO RAPIDLY, AS IF FILLING THE VOID LEFT BY HIS PARENTS' DEATHS...

...THAT HE SOON OUTGREW EVERY-THING THAT KATSU-NOSHIN COULD TEACH HIM.
BASED ON HIS AGE, THE MAN DETERMINED THAT HE COULD NOT TEACH HIS GRANDSON EVERYTHING.

KATSUNOSHIN TURNED TO HIS OLD FRIEND AND THE FOUNDER OF THE MAKABE ONE-HANDED STYLE, KAZUSHI MAKABE, TO INSTRUCT HIS GRANDSON.

THIS WAS MAMORU'S FIRST STEP ON THE PATH TO BECOMING A BLADE DEMON...

TEA ROOM
SIREN
KII (CREAK)
キィ…

KO (TOK)
コッ
KO
コッ

…
PASA (FLAP)
パサッ

THANKS FOR WAITING.

THERE'S A YOUNG GIRL HERE. IT'S AWFULLY LATE—

OH, SHE'S THE STAR OF THIS PLACE.
!?

ANYWAY, I TOOK A LOOK AT IT WHEN I HAD THE CHANCE DURING WORK— NOTHING TOO DEEP.
I APPRECIATE THAT.

BASED ON WHAT I SEE IN YOUR WRITING, YOU SEEM HONEST AND THOROUGH IN YOUR APPROACH.
SO I'LL TRUST YOU.

HOW MUCH CONFIDENCE DO YOU HAVE IN WHAT YOU'VE COLLECTED AND THE CONCLUSIONS YOU'RE DRAWING?

...I CAN'T BE SURE OF ANYTHING UNLESS I CHECK WITH HIM DIRECTLY.

BUT I BELIEVE THAT WHAT I'VE GOT IS ABOUT NINETY PERCENT TRUTH.

AFTER THAT, MAMORU SANK HIS LIFE INTO THE SWORD LIKE A SOUL POSSESSED.
THE OLDER STUDENTS FROM HIS DOJO CLAIM THAT HE UNDER-TOOK EVERY TRAINING METHOD HE COULD, REGARDLESS OF STYLE, EVEN ON HEARSAY.

WHEN HE HEARD ABOUT THE "TREE-STRIKING" EXERCISE OF THE JIGEN STYLE...
...HE DID IT ALL DAY LONG, UNTIL THE SKIN ON HIS PALMS HAD BEEN SCRAPED AWAY.

HE STOOD IN WAIST-DEEP POND WATER WHILE REPEATING HIS EXERCISES, TO BETTER STRENGTHEN HIS LOWER HALF.

AFTER HALF A DAY, THE LOSS OF WARMTH LEFT HIM SO EXHAUSTED, HE COULDN'T STAND.

A BOY WHO WAS NOT YET TEN YEARS OLD.
IN LATER YEARS, MAKABE WAS QUOTED AS SAYING...
"HE HAD BOTH THE APTITUDE AND THE UNYIELDING DRIVE TO ACHIEVE WHAT HE WANTED."

...IF THAT'S ALL TRUE, HE'S QUITE A CHARACTER ...
I PERFORMED AS MANY INTERVIEWS WITH OTHER STUDENTS AS I COULD.
UNLESS THEY'RE ALL LYING TOGETHER, I THINK WE CAN ASSUME IT'S THE TRUTH.
SO WHERE IS MAMORU HIJIKATA NOW?
I REALLY NEED TO MEET AND SPEAK WITH HIM IN PERSON.

FOR REASONS THAT I DON'T KNOW, HIJIKATA HAS LOST HIS VISION.

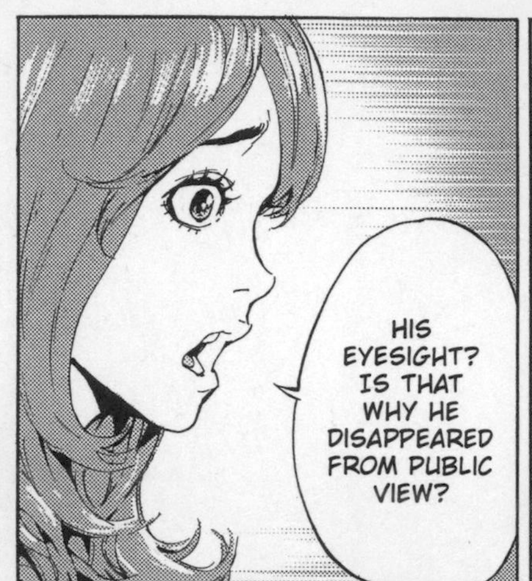
HIS EYESIGHT? IS THAT WHY HE DISAPPEARED FROM PUBLIC VIEW?

...

BUT HE STILL CONTINUES DOWN THE PATH HE'S CHARTED FOR HIMSELF.

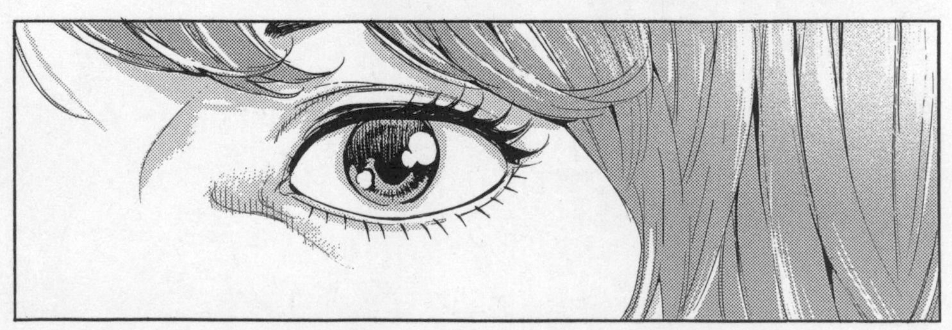

...

NO SURPRISE THIS TIME?

NO, NO SURPRISE.
I THINK THAT'S A PERFECTLY NATURAL CHOICE FOR HIM.

...

Until Death do us Part

PURURURU
(RRRR)
UNKNOWN NUMBER
PURURURU
DECLINE
ANSWER

... HELLO ...?

AGENT GENDA INFORMED ME THAT HE MIGHT HAVE SOMETHING INTERESTING TO SAY TONIGHT.

chapter 165
IF YOU'RE INTRIGUED, WHY DON'T YOU SIT IN?

IN ADDITION ...
...I HAVE A NUMBER OF OTHER ASSURANCES ABOUT HIJIKATA'S ACTIONS.

TWO YEARS LATER, HIS GRANDFATHER, KATSUNOSHIN, DIED, LEAVING HIM ENTIRELY ALONE IN THE WORLD.
BUT KAZUSHI MAKABE, WHO'D TAKEN A LIKING TO HIJIKATA, UNDERTOOK THE RARE STEP OF ACCEPTING HIM AS A PERMANENT APPRENTICE.
THE CONDITIONS WERE RIGHT FOR HIM TO COMPLETELY FOLLOW THE WAY OF THE SWORD.

ONE DAY, IN HIS SECOND YEAR OF MIDDLE SCHOOL—

?
...
HIJIKATA...

HEY... WHAT'S UP?

JUST THINKING... THERE REALLY IS SCUM IN THIS WORLD.

THE LOOK IN HIS EYES— IT WAS LIKE HE WAS STARING AT A STONE ON THE GROUND.

PERHAPS YOUNG MAMORU HIJIKATA TOOK UP THE SWORD BECAUSE HE WANTED TO KILL PEOPLE LIKE THAT DRUNKEN MAN.

BUT WHAT IF HE THEN REALIZED THAT SUCH PEOPLE WERE NOT WORTH HIS TIME OR TROUBLE?
...

...YET HE DIDN'T STOP.

THAT'S RIGHT. THIS PART IS ENTIRELY CONJECTURE— HIS REASON MIGHT BE DIFFERENT.
THE ACTIONS THAT HUMAN BEINGS TAKE CANNOT ALWAYS BE BOILED DOWN TO SHEER LOGIC.
PARTICULARLY WHEN YOU'RE TALKING ABOUT CHILDREN WHO ARE STILL GROWING AND MATURING.

AS A MATTER OF FACT, HE APPARENTLY PUT EVEN MORE EFFORT INTO THE SWORD AFTER THAT.

HIS TRAINING REGIMEN AT THE TIME WAS TEN THOUSAND SWINGS, MORNING AND NIGHT.
IN ORDER TO GIVE EACH AND EVERY SWING THE PROPER EFFORT, THIS PROCESS TOOK WELL OVER TWO HOURS.

SO THAT'S FOUR HOURS.
AND ANOTHER THREE HOURS FOR STANCE PRACTICE.

HE SWEATED IT OUT WITH THE ADULTS IN THE DOJO UNTIL EVENING, AND THEN DID HIS NIGHTTIME SET.
ANOTHER HOUR OF STRIKING TREES AFTER THE DOJO CLOSED.
APPARENTLY, HE DESTROYED A NUMBER OF GIANT CEDARS OUT BACK BEHIND THE DOJO.

TWO HOURS OF WEIGHT TRAINING.
TWO HOURS OF LEGWORK IN THE POND.
...

THAT'S FIFTEEN HOURS OF TRAINING PER DAY.

BUT... THAT DOESN'T ADD UP!
DIDN'T HE GO TO SCHOOL!? WHEN DID HE SLEEP IN THE REMAIN-ING NINE HOURS!?

I DON'T KNOW. GIVEN THAT EVERYONE NEEDS SLEEP...
...WE CAN IMAGINE THAT HE PROBABLY CAUGHT NAPS BETWEEN ACTIVITIES.

...I SEE... SO HE BECAME A DEMON OF THE BLADE BECAUSE HE WAS MEANT TO.

...THAT'S WHY HE CAN SLEEP WHEREVER HE WANTS ...

HERE'S ANOTHER ANECDOTE.
He's laying on the hook!
Takeda's trying to defend through it.
KAAN (CLANG)
That's the end of the fourth round! The fighters return to their corners.
WHERE ARE YOU GOING? WE'RE JUST GETTING TO THE GOOD STUFF.
THEY TURN THEIR BACKS LIKE THAT JUST AFTER THE BELL.
NOT EVEN CONCERNED ABOUT THE DANGER OF THE OPPONENT CHARGING THEIR BACKS.

OF COURSE NOT. IT'S A SPORT, NOT A SCHOOL OF COMBAT.
THAT CHAMPION FROM SOUTH AMERICA A WHILE BACK KEPT HIS SPIRIT TO HIM.
BUT THEY DON'T HAVE THAT!
UHH, I GUESS, BUT...

IF YOUR OPPONENT'S GOING TO FOLLOW THE RULES AT ANY AND ALL TIMES, THEN FINE.
BUT YOU NEVER KNOW WHEN A CAR MIGHT COME BARRELING DOWN ON YOU OUT OF NOWHERE.
I HAVE NO INTEREST IN A COMPETITOR WHO DOESN'T KEEP HIS WITS ABOUT HIM EVERY SECOND.

THAT'S WHEN I REALIZED THAT HE AND I HAD COMPLETELY DIFFERENT MINDSETS.
...
...HARUKA'S NOT AROUND...

OH, YEAH... SHE HAD SOMETHING TO DO.
WENT DOWN TO SIREN.

TO HER FRIEND'S PLACE?
SHE'LL BE FINE THERE, THEN.

HEY, MAMORU...

ABOUT THAT EXTREME RESTOCKING YOU JUST DID...

WHAT ARE YOU UP TO, MAN?

HAH... YOU'RE ON TO ME, HUH?
OF COURSE I AM!

THAT WENT BEYOND RESTOCKING!
ARE YOU ARMING AN ENTIRE TEAM OF YOUR OWN!?

JUST DON'T ASK ME WHY— I KNOW IT AIN'T RIGHT.
......

IF YOU FIND OUT WHY, SOME OF THE RESPONSIBILITY WILL FALL ON YOUR SHOULDERS.
THIS IS MY PROBLEM.

...IS IT ABOUT HARUKA...?

...

...

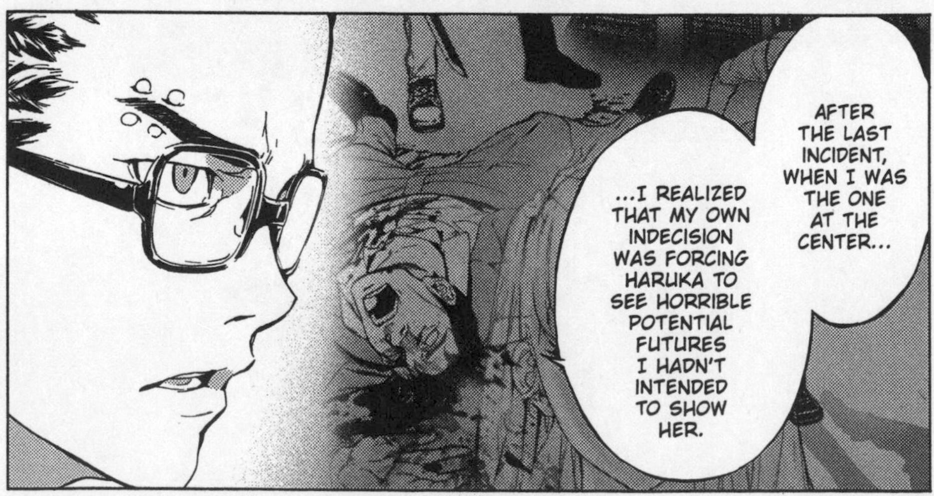
AFTER THE LAST INCIDENT, WHEN I WAS THE ONE AT THE CENTER...
...I REALIZED THAT MY OWN INDECISION WAS FORCING HARUKA TO SEE HORRIBLE POTENTIAL FUTURES I HADN'T INTENDED TO SHOW HER.

AS LONG AS SHE'S AROUND US, SHE HAS TO KEEP SEEING VISIONS OF YOU DYING OR KILLING OTHERS.
YOU REALIZE THAT, DON'T YOU!?

...

AND BECAUSE YOU KNOW THAT, YOU'VE BEEN HESITANT TO KEEP HER CLOSE BY, HAVEN'T YOU?

...I SEE... SO I WAS RIGHT...

EVEN I WAS A KID ONCE.

WHEN YOU SEE PEOPLE DYING, NASTY STUFF LIKE THAT, TOO EARLY ...
...YOU GROW UP REAL SCREWED UP, JUST LIKE ME.
IT AIN'T A GOOD THING.

ガタッ
GATA (THUNK)
I'M SORRY... I NEVER EVEN THOUGHT ABOUT OR CONSIDERED THESE THINGS.
AND YET I WAS IRRESPONSIBLE AND GOT CARRIED AWAY IN MY IGNORANCE.
I DON'T BLAME YOU. IT'S AN EXTREME SET OF CIRCUM-STANCES.
WHAT WOULD BE BEST IS IF HARUKA WERE MORE OF AN ADULT, AND CAPABLE OF CHOOSING ON HER OWN.
BUT I ACTUALLY WISH YOU'D NEVER REALIZED ANY OF THIS.
HUH?

SHE ONLY NEEDS ONE PESSIMIST HANGING AROUND.
IF BOTH OF US ARE JUST SITTING AROUND WITH THAT HANGDOG LOOK, SHE'S GONNA GET AGGRAVATED, DON'TCHA THINK?

HMM... I GUESS YOU'VE GOT A POINT...

I HAVE NO IDEA WHAT YOU'RE UP TO, BUT NOW THAT I'M AWARE OF IT, YOU GOTTA LET ME HELP!
I'M READY TO TAKE ON WHATEVER RESPONSIBILITY IS NECESSARY FOR HARUKA'S SAKE. I'LL WORK FOR FREE MY WHOLE LIFE, IF THAT'S WHAT IT TAKES.

...

...YOU MAKE A GOOD BIG BROTHER, IGAWA...

STILL NOT AS IMPORTANT AS A HUSBAND.
SHUT UP!

TEAROOM
SIREN

WHO ARE THEY?

Until Death do us Part

chapter 166

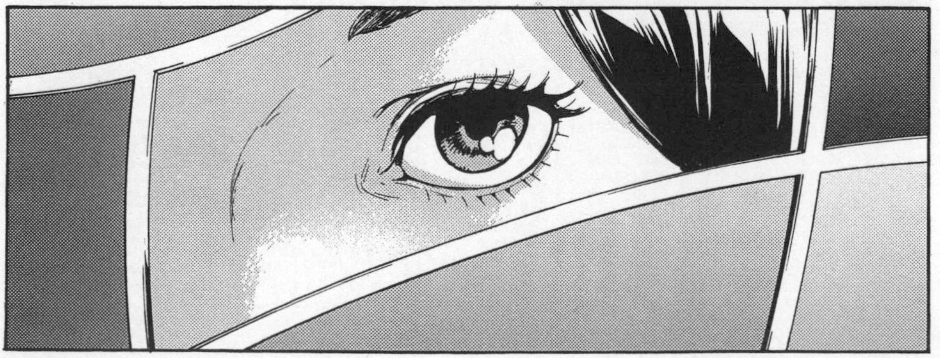

OH YES, THEY'RE OUT THERE.

...THOUGHT SO...

WHERE'S TATE-SAN?
WE CAN'T CALL MAMORU-SAN BECAUSE THE DETECTIVE IS IN HERE...

KARITO'S NOT HERE—HE HAD A NEW ASSIGNMENT TODAY.
MORE IMPORTANTLY...

...CAN YOU PREDICT THEIR OBJECTIVE?

...

THEY WANT THE WOMAN.

They're going to abduct her before she reaches the main street.
...

IF THAT'S IT, THERE'S NO NEED TO USE ANY KIND OF FORCE.
IN A WORST-CASE SCENARIO, WE CAN STILL ENSURE HER SAFETY BY REFUSING TO LET HER LEAVE.

DON'T WORRY— NO ONE HAS EVER ATTACKED THIS STORE AND LEFT UNHARMED.
IS... IS THAT SO?

If the future changes, let me know.
YES.

SPEAKING OF WHICH...

!?

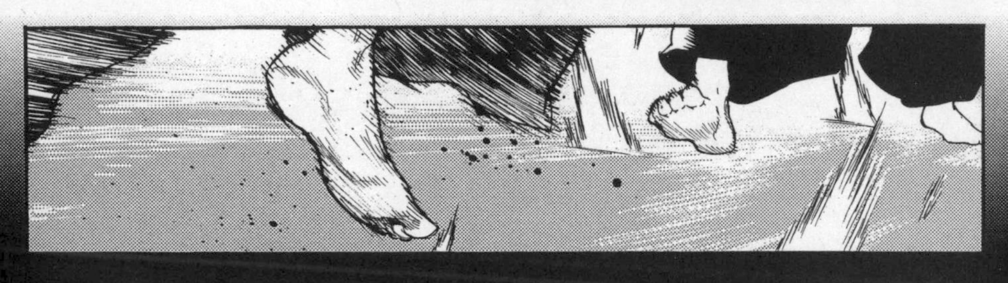

BA
(DUCK)
BUN
(WHOOSH)

BA
(FWAP)
WHAT THE...!?
...
TA
(TEK)

WHY WOULD YOU SWING FOR MY SHINS?
...YOU'RE NOT USING A NAGINATA OR ANYTHING.
YOU'RE REAL GOOD.
THERE'S NO WEAKNESS IN YOUR MINDSET—MUST BE BECAUSE YOU FIGHT TO APPREHEND CRIMINALS.
...

WHY ARE YOU SWINGING LIKE YOU DON'T CARE IF THE OPPONENT HITS YOU!?
IS IT BECAUSE THEY'RE ONLY USING A SHINAI!?
ISN'T SWORDPLAY PREDICATED UPON THE CONCEPT OF USING A REAL, DEADLY BLADE!?

HMPH... SO HE WAS TESTING ME.

SO THERE'S A STORY FROM MY OWN EXPE-RIENCE.
HE'S A NATURAL, THEN.
...IT'S EXACTLY HOW HE IS NOW...

LOOKING BACK ON THESE ANECDOTES, IT SEEMS HE SHUNNED ANY UNNECESSARY DISTRACTIONS FROM A VERY YOUNG AGE...
...SO THAT HE COULD FOCUS PURELY ON THE SWORD AND POLISH HIS SKILL AS A SWORDS-MAN.

WHAT'S YOUR OPINION OF THAT KIND OF LIFE?

...

...WELL...

HE MIGHT BE HAPPIER THAN ANYONE ELSE I KNOW.

DOING WHAT YOU LOVE AND SPENDING EVERY MOMENT OF YOUR LIFE IN ITS PURSUIT ...
...MIGHT MAKE YOU HAPPIER THAN ANYONE ELSE ON THE PLANET.
HUH!?
HAPPIER ???

EVEN IF IT MEANS ...
...THAT YOU WIND UP DYING IN A DITCH IN THE END.

...

AGENT GENDA... JUST LISTEN, DON'T TURN AROUND.
THERE ARE SOME FOREIGN MEN WATCHING THIS BUILDING OUT FRONT.

KARITO IS ABSENT TODAY, SO PLEASE BE CAREFUL.
PLUS...

PARDON ME.
SU (SHH)

OH! DO YOU MIND IF I ASK JUST ONE PERSONAL QUESTION?
HM? WHAT?

WHY DID YOU DECIDE TO BE A POLICE OFFICER?

NO BIG REASON... I JUST DON'T LIKE CRIMINALS.

KILLING, STEALING, TRAMPLING THE RIGHTS OF INNOCENT CIVILIANS.
I'M NOT A PATIENT OR FORGIVING ENOUGH MAN TO STAND BY AND LET IT HAPPEN.

THAT'S A GOOD ANSWER ...

ブォォォ…
BUOOO (VRMM)

スッ
SU (SHH)

WHAT'S UP? PROCURING MORE "TALENT"?
NO... JUST SOWING SEEDS THIS TIME.

THIS IS NOT AN OPPONENT WHO WILL BEHAVE AS WE WISH.

KON (KNOCK)
KON

KII (CREAK)
PARDON ME.

WHAT IS THIS PLACE!? WE'RE NOT GONNA FIND ANYONE HERE.

WATCH CLOSELY.

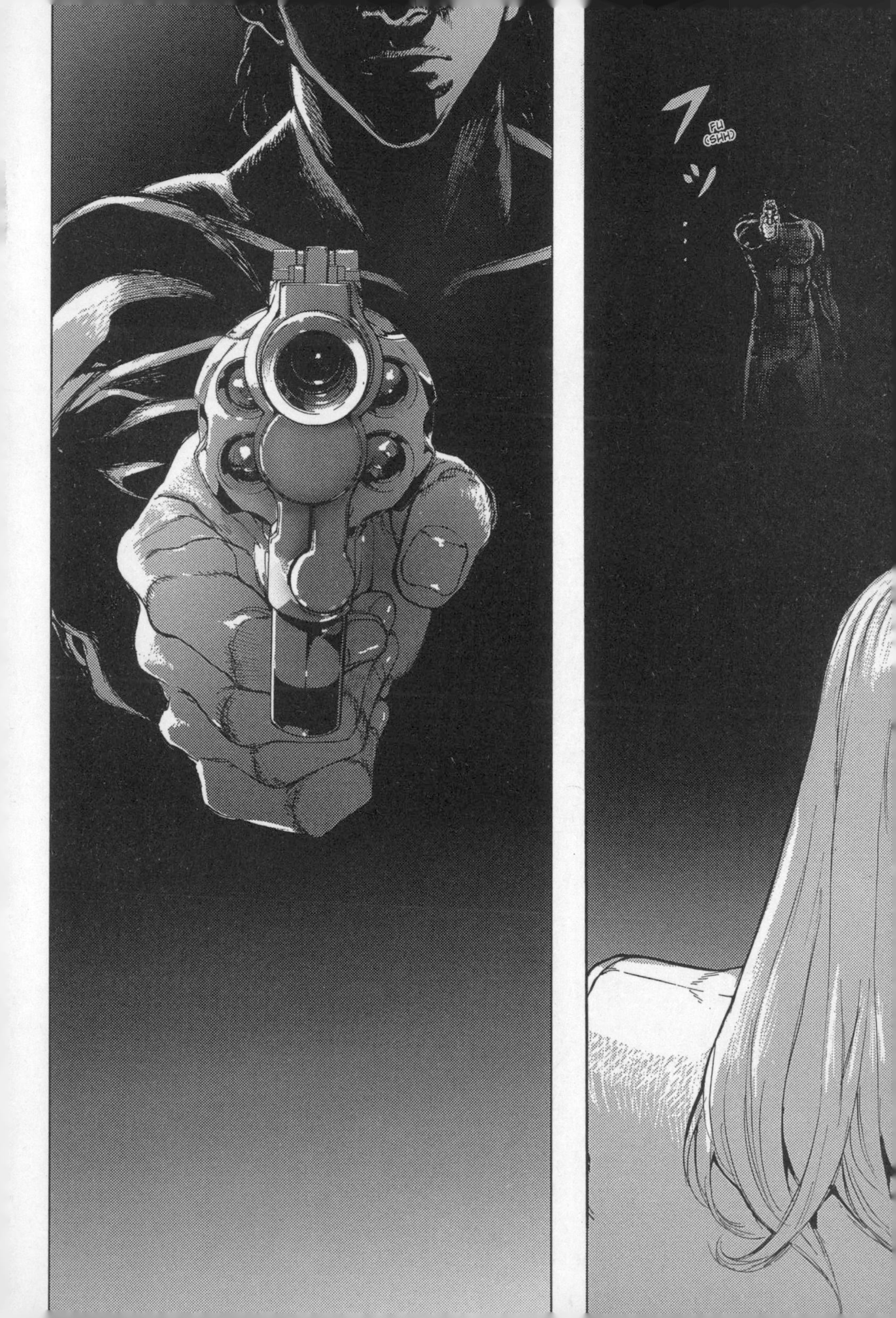
フッ
FU (SHH)

AAAH!

ONE WRONG MOVE AND YOU'RE DEAD. IF YOU GET TOO CLOSE WITHOUT RAISING ANY WARNING SOUND...
...HE'LL HAVE YOU DEAD BEFORE YOU EVEN KNOW IT.

WH-WH-WH... WHO IS THIS!?

HIS NAME IS JESUS.
THE GREATEST ASSASSIN IN THE WORLD.
!?
WAIT, "JESUS"!? LIKE... JESUS!?
HE TOOK ON A HEAVY INJURY PROTECTING HIS STUDENTS AFTER CRUSHING "24."
OLD GOOSE PUT HIM UP HERE SO HE COULD LAY LOW AND RECOVER.

*DANTE 313: A TRANSPLANT CONNECTION PLOT TO ABDUCT WOMEN AND FERTILIZE THEM, THEN HARVEST THE BABIES FOR ORGANS. IRONICALLY, THIS PLAN WAS HATCHED BECAUSE JESUS PUSHED THE TPC TO DESPERATION.

I, ON THE OTHER HAND, THINK I'VE GOT THE SITUATION COMPETELY FIGURED OUT.

SO LONG.

SO WHAT'S THE PLAN?
WAS THAT ALL YOU NEEDED TO DO?

IT WAS MORE THAN ENOUGH. HE'S GOING TO ACT. IT JUST WON'T BE WHAT WE EXPECT.
AND IT MOST CERTAINLY SUITS OUR PURPOSES NOT TO BE INVOLVED WITH HIS ACTIONS.

HE'S THE WILD CARD IN THIS SCENARIO.

AND NOW, WE'VE GOT SOME OTHER CARDS TO PREPARE.

UH... HUH?

BUOOO (VRRRM)

...DANTE 313...
A HELL OF MY OWN CREATION ...

chapter 167

SO YOU'RE SAYING YOU NEVER GOT THAT BOMB IN YOUR TOOTH REMOVED? IT'S STILL IN THERE!?

IT WAS MEANT AS A SAFEGUARD AGAINST BETRAYAL.
THEY STUCK IT DEEP IN THE GUMS TO PREVENT EASY REMOVAL. IF WE GET TOO CUTE TRYING TO PULL IT OUT, IT COULD GO OFF.

IF THEY FIND OUT I'VE REMOVED IT, GENIE WILL STOP TRUSTING ME, AND OUR PLAN GOES UP IN SMOKE.
ALL THIS TROUBLE FOR NOTHING.
NOPE! IT'S A DEED THAT SYMBOLIZES MY TRUST-WORTHI-NESS.
OH, COME ON! IT SHOULD BE POSSIBLE WITH ENOUGH TIME!
YOU KNOW THE NETWORK'S GOT THE RESOURCES TO REMOVE IT!

THIS IS RIDICU-LOUS...

RIDICULOUS OR NOT, HE NEEDS TO HAVE CONTROL OVER MY LIFE AS THE ACE UP HIS SLEEVE.
IT PROTECTS AGAINST TREACHERY AND IS A MEASURE OF SILENCE IF WE FAIL.
WITHOUT THOSE THINGS, HE COMES TO RUIN.

UNBE-
LIEVABLE
...
...

ANYWAY,
DOESN'T IT
HURT?

YEAH...
IT'S BEEN
IMPACTING THE
NERVE EVER
SINCE THEY
PUT IT IN.
DRIVING ME UP
THE WALL...
HAVE YOU
NOTICED ME
BEING MORE
IRRITABLE
LATELY?

YOU'RE
ALWAYS
IRRITABLE.

ピッ
PI
(BEEP)
!?

This is Haruka. Is Mamoru-san there!?
ile Edit View Info Hel
start
haruka online
Off Line
Off Line
Off Line

WHAT IS IT?

TEA ROOM
SIREN

...THERE THEY ARE....

I'M OFF DUTY AND UNARMED.
IF THEY'RE PACKING, THAT MEANS TROUBLE.

BUT SINCE THEY HAVEN'T INVADED YET, THAT MEANS THEY DON'T WANT TO USE FORCE.
EITHER THEY KNOW WHAT KIND OF PLACE "SIREN" IS, OR THEY'RE WAITING FOR MORE MEN...

I NEVER DETECTED THAT I WAS BEING FOLLOWED ...
...SO THAT WOULD SUGGEST THEIR TARGET IS SOMEONE ELSE WITHIN THE BUILDING ...

...

IF WE EXCLUDE THE USUAL STAFF, THAT LEAVES ...

WELL, IT WOULD ONLY LEAVE THIS WOMAN AS THEIR TARGET.
...
KA (TOK)
KA
OH?
...UMM...
JUST A MOMENT.

I'VE BEEN HOPING TO SEE YOU, MISS.

!?
???
...

I THOUGHT I SAW YOUR HAIR POKING OUT FROM THE BOOTH—AND IT TURNS OUT TO BE THE MISSING GIRL.

DO I HAVE THAT RIGHT, HARUKA TOOYAMA-SAN?

Er... um... I...
I SEE... IT'S AGENT GENDA.
THE DETEC-TIVE?

YEAH. HE'S A REAL PAIN IN THE ASS.
BUT YOU CRUSHED HIM LAST TIME.

DON'T BE STUPID— I JUST BARELY WON THAT ONE.
IN FACT, AGENT GENDA'S SWING WAS JUST A HALF-BREATH QUICKER THAN MINE.
IF I HADN'T BEEN GOING FOR THE "BLADE-CHIPPER" FROM THE START, IT WOULD HAVE BEEN ME WITH HIS FOREHEAD SPLIT OPEN.

I ONLY WON BECAUSE MY WEAPON WAS "DANZAI," MY BLADE, WHILE HE WAS USING A SIMPLE POLICE BATON.

OH... REALLY?
...
SO THAT MEANS IT WOULD BE FOOLISH TO JUST WANDER IN THERE.

BUT WE CAN'T JUST IGNORE THE FACT THAT THE WOMAN'S BEEN TARGETED...
OUGHT TO STAKE OUT A LOCATION NEARBY, JUST IN CASE.
ALL RIGHT.

HOTEL INNO

BOURBON.
CRUSHED ICE.
HUH?

YOU DON'T LOOK HAPPY.

...

I DON'T APPRECIATE THAT EYESORE STANDING AROUND.

...

OF COURSE.

KO (TOK)
KO

SHALL WE BEGIN NEGOTIA-TIONS?
I HAVE THE MOST BOORISH VISITORS TONIGHT.

I APOLOGIZE FOR THAT. HOW'S YOUR INJURY COMING ALONG?

SHOULD BE FULLY BACK TO NORMAL WITHIN A MONTH.
THAT'S GOOD.

EVEN THOUGH I WAS A PAWN ON THE LOSING SIDE, I WON'T COME CHEAP.
THAT'S FINE.

ARE YOU GOING TO MAKE IT WORTH MY WHILE?

HMM?
THE LAST JOB GOT ME TERRIBLY STRESSED OUT.

WE CAN'T HAVE ENOUGH HANDS ON DECK FOR THIS ONE.
IT'S LIKELY TO INVOLVE MORE THAN JUST SNIPING ON YOUR END.

AND WHAT'S THE GOAL?

THERE ARE A NUMBER OF THINGS WE STAND TO GAIN, BUT I SUSPECT WHAT YOU'LL FIND MOST INTRIGUING IS...

?

...THE FREEDOM OF BLACKS FROM THE YOKE OF OPPRESSION, PERHAPS?

...GO ON, TELL ME MORE...
コト
KOTO (TUNK)

I HAD A FEELING YOU'D BITE AT THAT ONE.

TEAROOM
SIREN

STAFF ONLY

KATA (TAP)
カタ
KATA
カタ
KATA
カタ
DRY

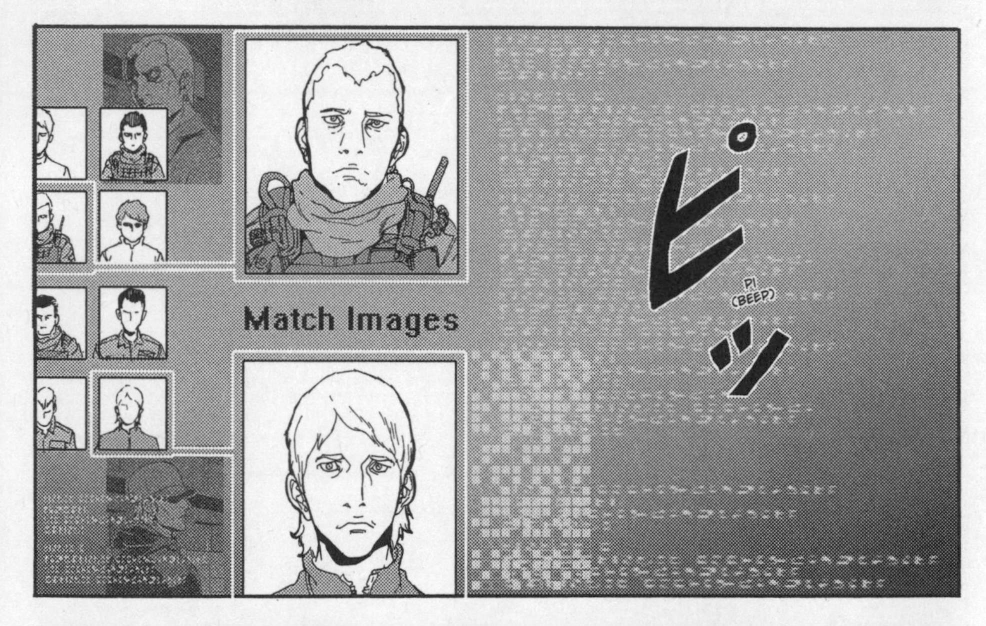
Match Images
ピッ
PI (BEEP)

I KNEW IT...
THEY'RE BOTH FORMER MEMBERS OF "BLACK FIRE," THE NOW-BANKRUPT PRIVATE MILITARY CONTRACTOR.
BLACK FIRE

BLACK FIRE
BLACK FIRE
MEMBERS OF THE TEAM THAT INDISCRIMINATELY FIRED INTO A CROWD WHILE ON DUTY IN IRAQ, SLAUGHTERING DOZENS OF INNOCENT CIVILIANS FOR NO REASON.

AFTER THE COMPANY'S LICENSE WAS STRIPPED AWAY, THE ENTIRE TEAM WENT FULLY CRIMINAL.

THEY'RE DANGEROUS MEN...

WHAT'S GOING ON?

NOTHING FOR THE MOMENT, BUT WE'VE GOT THE PLACE SURROUNDED.
WE CAN TAKE HER AS SOON AS SHE STEPS OUT THE DOOR.

SO WHAT MAKES THIS WOMAN WORTHWHILE, EH?

SHE'S COLLECTING INFORMATION ON THE GUY WITH THE HUNDRED-MILLION-DOLLAR BOUNTY ON HIS HEAD.
WANTED
SHE'S BEEN SNIFFING AROUND ENOUGH THAT OTHER FOLKS LIKE US WILL BE AFTER THE INTEL.
WE'VE GOT TO GET OUR HANDS ON THAT BEFORE THEY DO.

SOUNDS LIKE A SOLID PLAN TO ME, CAPTAIN.
WE NEED COLD, HARD CASH TO KEEP THE COMPANY RUNNING NOW THAT WE'RE ESSENTIALLY OUT OF WORK.

I DUNNO, IT'S A TRICKY PLACE SHE'S FOUND FOR HERSELF.

BREAK DOWN THE DOOR, AND WE'LL HAVE AEGIS TO DEAL WITH.
AND IF WE TAKE TOO LONG, ANY ONE OF THE OTHER BOUNTY HUNTERS WILL COME ALONG.

THERE IT IS.
WHAT'S IN THE BAG?

JIII
(ZIP)

AN AA-12 AUTOMATIC SHOTGUN.

AEGIS DOESN'T STAND A CHANCE AGAINST THIS BABY.
A FEW DOZEN SHOTGUN BLASTS WILL TEAR THROUGH HIS PRECIOUS METAL ARM LIKE A HOT KNIFE THROUGH BUTTER.
EVEN THE SAMURAI WILL GET SHREDDED LIKE A RAG DOLL.

SO WE'RE DOING THIS, THEN?

OF COURSE. WE CAN EVEN TEST OUT THE GUN'S LETHALITY ON ANYONE ELSE INSIDE THE BUILDING.
chapter 168

...

IS HE TREATING YOU WELL?

UH-OHHH...

!?

I KNEW HIM, BUT I DIDN'T UNDERSTAND HIM. I'VE BEEN LEARNING ALL KINDS OF THINGS ABOUT HIM TONIGHT.
I ALWAYS THOUGHT HE WAS A COLD BASTARD WHO CARED FOR NOTHING BUT HIS SWORD...

...BUT GIVEN THAT HE'S WATCHING OUT FOR YOU, I GUESS THAT'S NOT ENTIRELY THE CASE.
...
...?

I'M SORRY THAT THE POLICE WEREN'T ANY HELP...
...WITH WHAT HAPPENED TO YOUR PARENTS.
...
DE... TECTIVE ...?
AH!

THE FUTURE... JUST CHANGED ...

...
THEY'RE COMING ...

WE'RE ENTIRELY WORTHLESS AT OUR JOB...
...IF WE CAN'T EVEN EASE A POOR GIRL'S FEARS AT A TIME LIKE THIS.

BUT I'VE STILL GOT A JOB TO DO.
SU... (SHH)

TODAY MIGHT BE MY LAST. I'M GLAD I COULD SHED SOME REGRETS.

UM ...
WHAT DO YOU MEAN?
...

!?
NO, YOU CAN'T GO!!

IF YOU JUST WAIT A MINUTE ...

THEN HE'LL BE HERE?
THAT WON'T FLY! A PROPER COP DOESN'T LET A CRIMINAL DO HIS JOB FOR HIM.

BESIDES, HE WON'T BE IN TIME, WILL HE?
THIS IS WHEN YOU NEED A DETECTIVE ON YOUR SIDE.

PLUS, I HAVE A DUTY TO PROTECT AND SERVE.
???

NO, YOU CAN'T!!

!?

BUOOO (VRMMM)
Ma-moru-san!

Come quick! The detective's going out on his own!
They're going to shoot him!!

IGA-WA!
I'M ON IT!
BUOOO

THAT'S RIGHT... THEY'RE NOT AFTER ME...
SO YOU'RE GOING TO HANG BACK AND WATCH WHAT HAPPENS, YEAH?

KA (TOK)
カッ
KA
カッ

EITHER OF YOU GOT A LIGHT?

TAKE THE INITIATIVE AND CATCH THEM OFF GUARD.

NO. FUCK OFF!

YOU DON'T HAVE TO BE AN ASSHOLE.
GOSO (RUSTLE)
GOSO

OH!?

FOUND ONE.

HYU
(SWISH)
?
DOSA
(THWAKK)
WHAT
...?
DOSA
(THUMP)

DOGA
(WHAM)

DOSU
(THUD)
CHA
(CLICK)
STOP RIGHT THERE!!

KA
(TAK)
PASHU
(PSHAT)

GOTTA TAKE THEM DOWN BEFORE BACKUP ARRIVES!
!?
!

YOU CROOKS...

...WILL NEVER STOP ME!!

DADA (DASH)
KIKII (SCREECH)
TA (TEK)

BAKI (CRUNCH)

GAH!
DOKA (THUMP)
HNG!
BAKI
GWUH!

WHAT'S GOING ON!?
DA
DA
...AGENT GENDA...
...YO...

YOU'RE A LITTLE LATE.
BUT YOU BROKE THE STALEMATE BETWEEN ME AND THEM. THANKS.

...YOU SOUND LIKE SHIT...
DID THEY GET YOU!?

NOTHING TOO BAD. TAKE CARE OF HIM, WILL YOU?
TON (SHOVE)

SURE ...
DOSU (WHUDD)

DOSA
(THUMP)

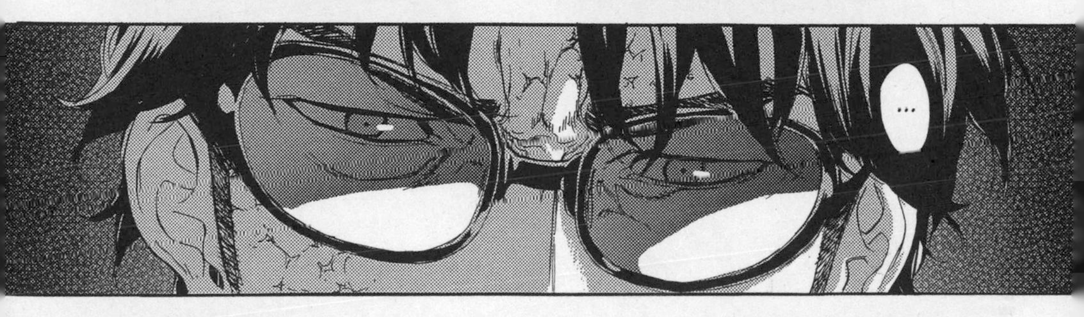
...

BA
(LEAP)

WHERE IS HE!?

!?

AH ...

YO.
LITTLE MISS...
SEEMS LIKE EVERYONE'S ALL RIGHT.

GFHK!

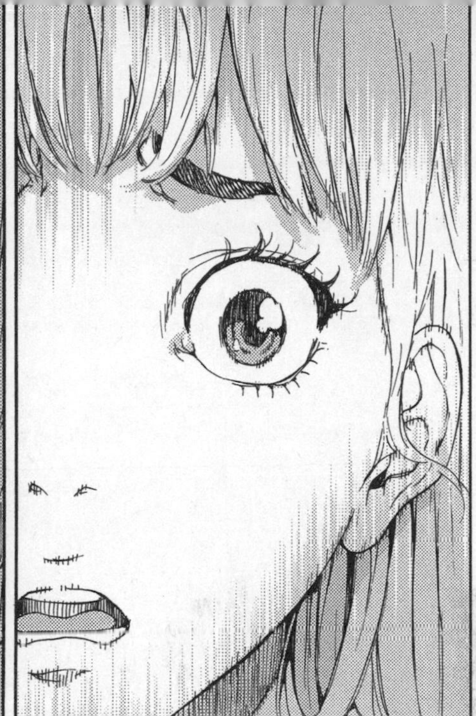

WAIT, DETECTIVE...
DON'T GO!

YOU CAN'T!
...
COME BACK!

AH, DAMN...

DON'T CRY, LITTLE MISS...
YOU LOOK LIKE A WRECK.
I CAN'T HELP IT.

I KNEW THIS WAS MY TIME TO DIE.

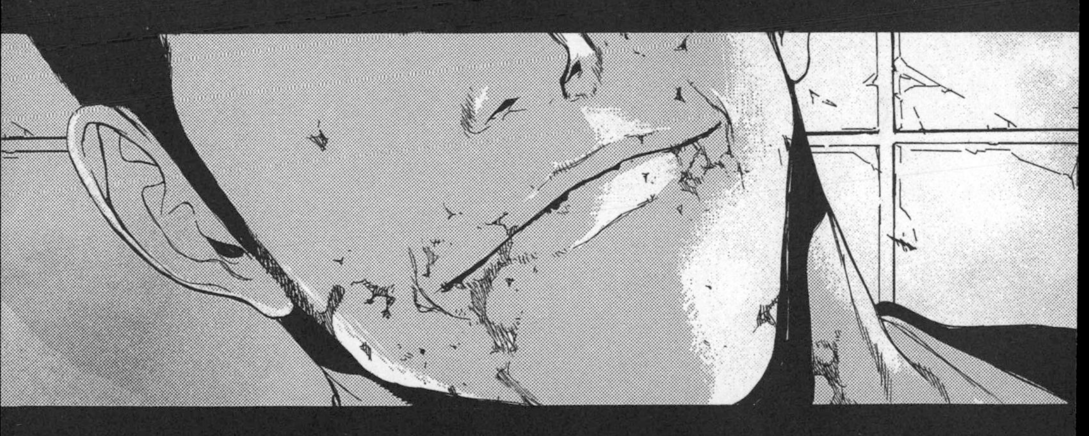

BY MY STANDARDS, THAT'S PRETTY GOOD.

WAAAAAH!!
AAAAH!!

DON'T CRY!
AGENT GENDA DID EXACTLY WHAT HIS JOB DICTATED.
IF ANYTHING, HE'S HAPPY ABOUT IT.

DOING WHAT YOU LOVE AND SPENDING EVERY MOMENT OF YOUR LIFE IN ITS PURSUIT ...
...MIGHT MAKE YOU HAPPIER THAN ANYONE ELSE ON THE PLANET.

EVEN IF IT MEANS THAT YOU WIND UP DYING IN A DITCH IN THE END.

Until Death do us Part

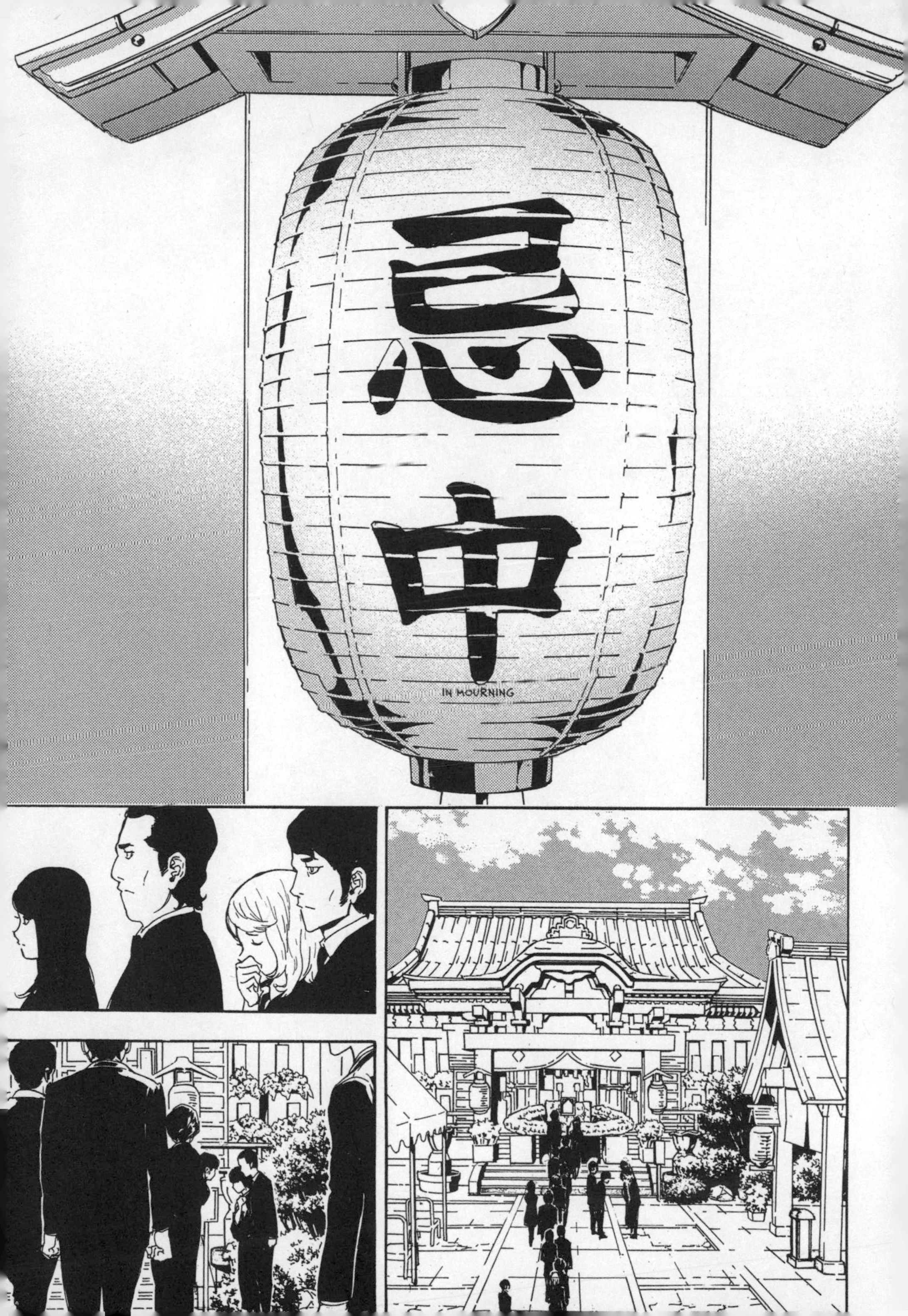
忌中
IN MOURNING

chapter 169

MASUDA-SAN...

WHY AREN'T YOU DRESSED IN BLACK, HORIKAWA!?

I SWORE I WOULDN'T SAY MY FAREWELLS TO GENDA-SAN UNTIL I CAUGHT THE GUYS WHO GOT AWAY.

AND ON THAT TOPIC, I'VE GOT WORD OF A HOTEL WHERE SOME MEN WHO FIT THE DESCRIPTION ARE HANGING OUT.
FEEL LIKE JOINING ME? I'VE GOT SOME OTHER OFFICERS IN ON THE OPERATION.

... LISTEN TO YOU ...
...

ALL RIGHT.
I'LL MEET UP WITH YOU SOON.

GENDA-SAN...
GET SOME REST. WE'RE GOING TO MAKE UP FOR YOUR ABSENCE.

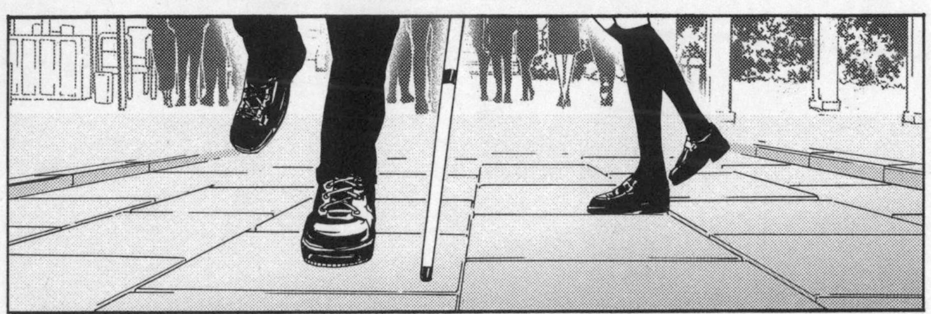

YOU'RE REALLY GOING, AREN'T YOU...?
HMPH... NO USE TRYING TO KEEP SECRETS FROM YOU, I SUPPOSE.

YOU CAME HERE TODAY TO APOLOGIZE TO AGENT GENDA, RIGHT?
......
I UNDER-STAND THAT I CAN'T STOP YOU.
WE COULD ALL TRY, AND YOU'D BREAK THROUGH US ANYWAY!
THAT'S EXACTLY RIGHT...

EVEN IGAWA-SAN IS GETTING INTO THIS FOR MY SAKE...
THAT WAS HIS WISH. I KNOW IT'S HARD TO DO THIS, BUT YOU SHOULDN'T LET IT BOTHER YOU.

!?

HEY... WHAT'S THIS ABOUT?

THEN I'LL BE THE NEXT ONE TO CHALLENGE YOU, MAMORU HIJIKATA!!
AND I KNOW I CAN WIN!!

タッ
TA (TEK)

...I'LL BE DAMNED...
AND WHAT DOES SHE MEAN BY "WIN"?

POLICE HOSPI-TAL

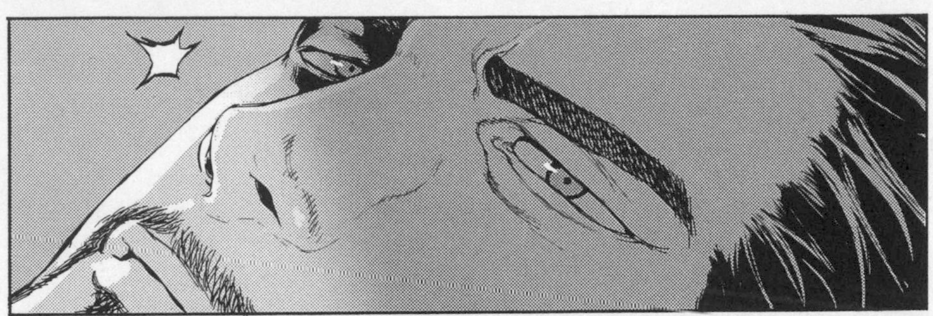

!?

BA
(FWAP)
HNK
!?
!?

WH-WHO ARE YOU!?
YOU IDIOT!

I LET YOU WALK ON PURPOSE.
BUT GETTING CAUGHT JUST RUINS OUR ENTIRE PLAN!

WHA...?
WH-WH-WH-WHA...?

CAN'T YOU EVEN PROTECT YOURSELF, YOU USELESS LUMP!?

SO WE'RE GONNA TAKE CUSTODY OF YOU FOR A LITTLE WHILE.

DON'T ASSUME YOU'LL HAVE ANY FREEDOM FOR NOW!!

AREN'T YOU ALL GENIE'S MEN!?
WHY ARE YOU LETTING HIM WALK AROUND!?

SORRY. WE'RE WORKIN' FOR HIM NOW.
WHAT !?

WE WERE UNDER NO OBLIGATION TO OBEY YOUR ORDERS TO BEGIN WITH.
SO LET'S ALL PLAY NICE AND DO WHAT HE SAYS, YEAH?

...

HEH!

...YOU...
YOU SHAMELESS...

LET'S ESCORT MR. TURUS DOWN TO THE HOLD.

...THE HOLD!?

GACHA (CHUNK)
ガチャ

...
SORRY FOR THE SHORT NOTICE, BUT YOU'RE WORKING FOR US NOW.

THIS IS ON GENIE'S ORDERS.

BUT TECHNICALLY, YOU CAN THINK OF YOURSELVES AS MY OVER-SEERS.
YOU'RE SUPPOSED TO MAKE SURE I DON'T BETRAY YOU.

...

I SEE.
SO WE'RE SUPPOSED TO HEAL UP TO GET BACK IN ACTION THROUGH THIS LONG VOYAGE?
...THAT'S EXACTLY RIGHT...

AND SINCE YOU'RE TAGGING ALONG, YOU'VE GOT TO MAKE YOURSELF USEFUL TOO.

YEAH, I KNOW.

I WOULD HAVE JUST WASTED AWAY IF I'D BEEN STUCK IN PRISON THIS WHOLE TIME.
DON'T WANNA ACTUALLY TURN INTO A REAL "DONICHI."

WHAT?

NOTHIN', JUST A PRIVATE JOKE.

I DUNNO WHAT'S GOTTEN INTO YOU, BUT YOU'VE GOT MY ASSISTANCE FOR SAVING ME.
I CAN BE USEFUL.

BUT AS SOON AS WE'RE DONE, I'M TAKIN' OFF.
GOT IT, BOSS?

...WHAT-EVER YOU WANT...

A SHORT WHILE AGO—
I'VE BEEN WAITING FOR YOU.
...SENJI-SAN...

THE BIG GUY TOLD ME TO HANDLE THE REST.
SO FROM THIS POINT ON, I'LL BE YOUR BODYGUARD, LITTLE MISS.
...
I SUPPOSE NOTHING I SAY WILL CHANGE YOUR MIND.
BUT...
PLEASE DON'T TURN ME DOWN. I'M ONLY HERE BECAUSE I COULDN'T BE THERE.
AND THERE'S NOTHING LEFT FOR ME ASIDE FROM THIS ROLE.
I'LL BE AT YOUR SIDE, ALIVE OR DEAD, UNTIL HE COMES BACK.

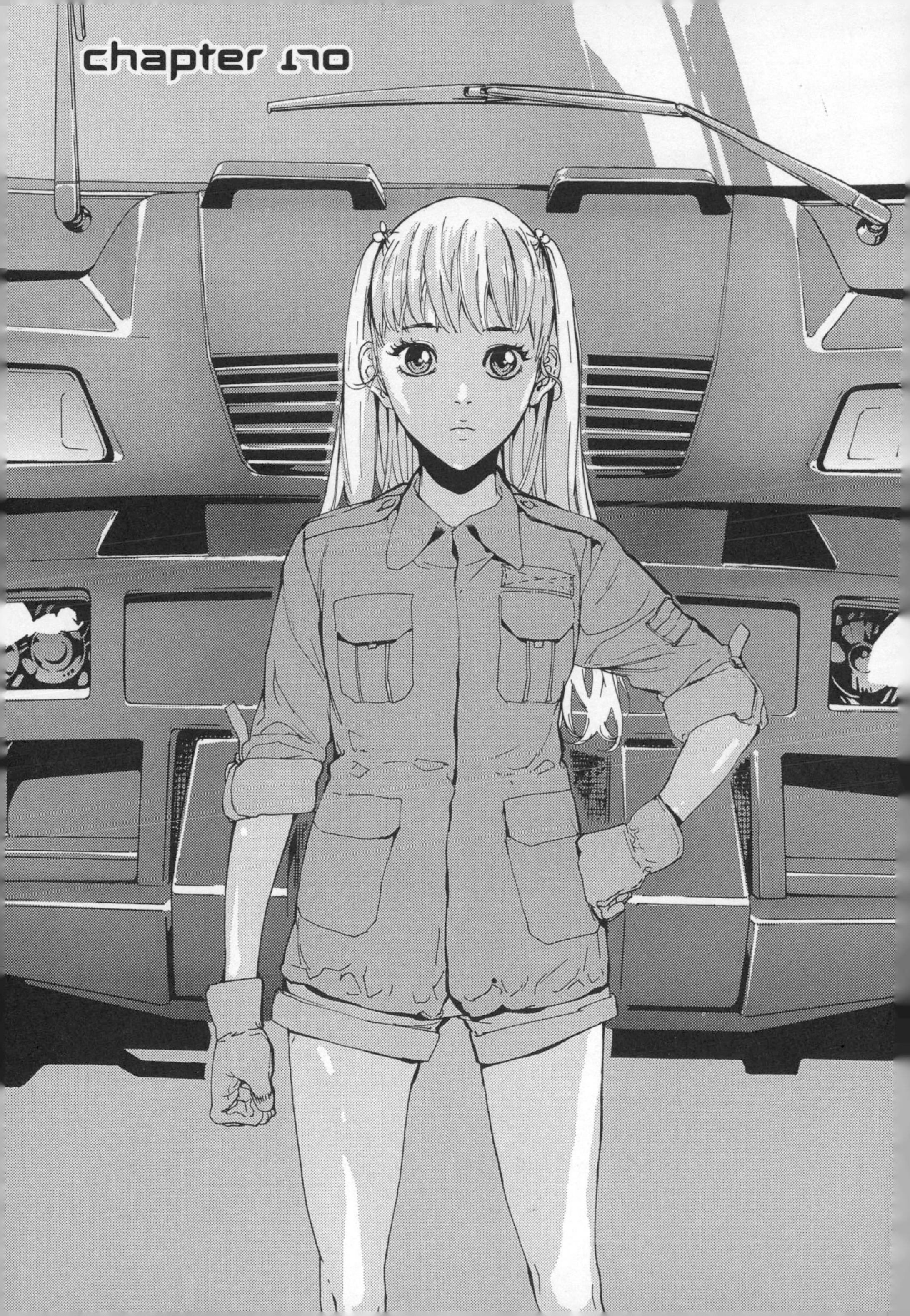
chapter 170

I SUPPOSE WE MUST CONDITION-ALLY ACCEPT.

Master, I received two requests for leave via the Net thirty seconds ago.

There is more information I have not relayed to you.
It is extremely private information, and therefore I was planning to process it by myself, as long as the circum-stances allowed.
However, I have now identified it as crucial information and will therefore reveal it to you.

MAMORU HIJIKATA AND HARUKA TOOYAMA ARE FUTURE HUSBAND AND WIFE???
Yes.

UMM...
...ERRR...

GEEZ, THIS IS A MESS!
ボ BORI (SCRATCH)
ボリ
リ BORI

Master, those are not the words of a 24-year-old adult.
YES, I'M SORRY.
MY ESTIMATED MENTAL AGE IS STILL ELEVEN. MY MIND HASN'T CHANGED FROM THE DAY MY MOTHER WAS KILLED.
I ONLY PRETEND TO ACT OLDER AS MY BODY AGES.

...
I don't see it that way, Master.

SPARKY, HARUKA TOOYAMA HERSELF WOULD NOT BE ENOUGH TO RESTRAIN HIM.
Yes, Master.

I NEED TO THINK OF A WAY TO PENALIZE HIM.

Announcing the consensus decision of the Element Network.
BEEP!

Blade
Igawa
As of today, Mamoru Hijikata and Ryoutarou Igawa have left the Network.

WH- WHAT'S THAT?

...

Therefore, Team "Blade" is no longer functional ...
...and is hereby reassigned into Team "Bucephalus."

HUH!?

An official announcement will be made upon Haruka Tooyama's return.

WHAT DOES THIS MEAN!?

IT MEANS TEAM "BLADE" IS NOW DEFUNCT.
IT'S LOST ITS ACTIVE MEMBERS AND OPERATOR.

SO HARUKA'S ON OUR TEAM NOW?
I SUPPOSE THAT'S RIGHT.

ブオオオ
BUOOO (VRMMM)

YOU WERE AT AGENT GENDA'S FUNERAL, WEREN'T YOU?
...YES...

IT MUST HAVE GIVEN HIM SOMETHING TO THINK ABOUT.
YOUR PAL SPED UP THE PLAN RIGHT AFTER THE COP DIED IN THE LINE OF DUTY.

HUH!?

IT WASN'T SUPPOSED TO GO INTO EFFECT FOR ANOTHER MONTH.

...

PERHAPS IT WAS...

YOU GOT TO WITNESS AGENT GENDA AT HIS BEST.

BUT PEOPLE DIE WHEN IT'S TIME TO DIE, AND THERE'S NO MEANING TO IT.
THE ONLY THING THAT MAKES IT MEANINGFUL IS THE WILL OF THE PEOPLE WHO LIVE ON AFTER THAT!
...MAMORU-SAN...
...

BUOOO (VRMM)

KIKI (SCREECH)
!?

GACHA (CLICK)
HEY! HEY!
NO OUT-SIDERS IN HERE, YOU KNOW THAT!!

NICE TO SEE YOU AGAIN.
HUH? IT'S YOU...

I'M SORRY FOR ACTING WITHOUT PERMISSION.

OH, WE HAVE A GUEST?
IS HE A NEW MEMBER?

NO, HE'S A YAKUZA AND AN OUTSIDER!
SENJI TAMAGAWA, **FORMER** YAKUZA. A PLEASURE.

HMM... I LIKE THE WAY HE LOOKS...
HOW SO!?

NOT HIS FACE! I MEAN HIS EXPERIENCE.
A GOOD WOMAN UNDERSTANDS THESE THINGS.

PARDON THE INTER-RUPTION.

PYRO-SAN.
LOTS OF VISITORS TODAY.
KON (TAP)
KON
WE'VE GOT NOTICE OF REASSIGNMENT.
AS OF TODAY, "BUCEPHALUS" IS NO MORE. ITS MEMBERS ARE IN A NEW TEAM.
THIS AREA WILL REVERT TO THE PURVIEW OF TEAM "ALCBANE," THE FORMER GROUP IN CHARGE.
WHAT!? WHY DIDN'T ANYONE TELL US THIS STUFF!?

OUR NEW GROUP, THE INTER-NATIONAL STRIKE TEAM "UDDUP"...
...IS PLACED UNDER THE LEADERSHIP OF HARUKA TOOYAMA.

YES, SIR!

ONE OF THE THREE NEW MEMBERS IS...

...THIS TALENTED FELLOW, CODE-NAMED "SHOT."
I REMEMBER SHOT—HE WAS THE ELITE SOLDIER IN CHARGE OF SOUTH AFRICA.

AS OF TODAY, I'M UNDER YOUR COMMAND.
N-NICE TO MEET YOU.
NEXT IS "ELAN."
ELAN'S ON THE WAY OVER AS WE SPEAK.

AND LASTLY, "SPARC."
OUR OPERATOR.
HUH !?

SPARC
speaking
Spiron
I will be under-taking my duties here while simulta-neously seeing to other work...
...but I hope you do not mind this.

IF YOU NEED MORE MEMBERS, THAT WILL BE AT THE LEADER'S DISCRETION.
REQUEST MORE, AND WE'LL HAVE OTHER AGENTS READY TO JOIN.
???
...

SU (SHH)
スッ

...AND WHAT CAN YOU DO?

I'M THE YOUNG LADY'S BULLET SHIELD.
SOUNDS GOOD...I'M SURE YOU'LL LIVE UP TO THE TASK.
NICE ATTITUDE.
A PLEASURE TO BE ON THE TEAM.

TAKE ME WITH YOU.
I CAN BE OF GREAT HELP TO YOU.

BUT AREN'T YOU A MEMBER OF THE NETWORK ...?

THE BOSS IS BACK IN ACTION, SO I'M OUT OF A POSITION AS OF TODAY.
AND I WAS JUST THINKING OF TAKING A VACATION TO AFRICA ANYWAY.

...TH... THANK YOU...SO MUCH...

GEEZ, EVERY-ONE'S GETTING INVOLVED ...

SO YOU'D BETTER KEEP UP, OR GET LEFT IN THE DUST.

DAAH!! SHUT UP ALREADY !!
I'M THE ACE OF THE TEAM! I PULL MY OWN WEIGHT!

OUR DUTY IS TO INFILTRATE DUHANA AND TRACK DOWN A CRIMINAL.

THE TARGET— "BLADE."
!?

FOR THE NEXT MONTH AND CHANGE, AS BLADE'S SHIP HEADS TO ITS DESTINATION ...

...WE WILL BE IN A JOINT TRAINING PERIOD TO ENSURE THE GROUP WORKS AS A TEAM.

...

THIS IS MY TEAM...

I WON'T LET ANY OF THEM DIE...

Until Death do us Part

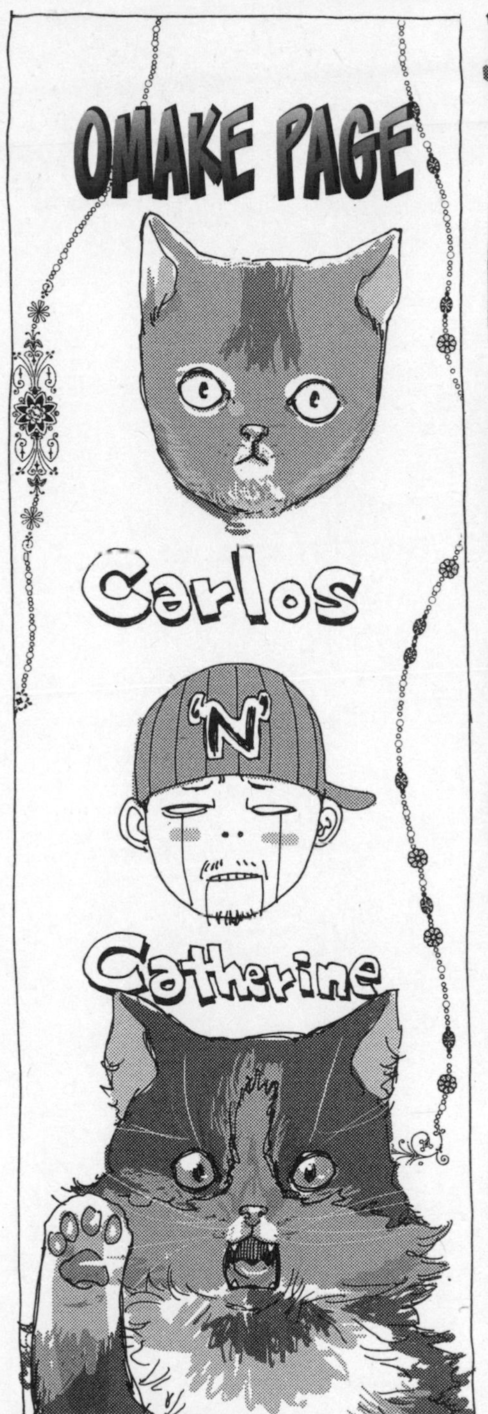
OMAKE PAGE
Carlos
'N'
Catherine

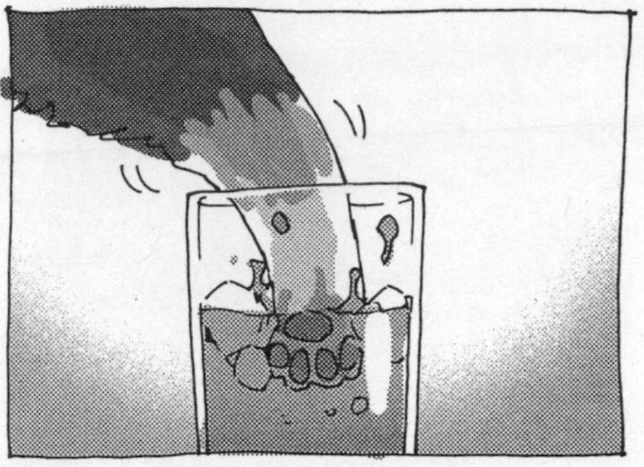

MMM... AMERICANO.

MMM... AMERI-CANO.

HM?
WHAT'S UP, CARLOS?

MEOWW! ♡

THAT'S RIGHT, CARLOS! IT'S YOUR BIG BRO!

UH...
FALLS FOR IT EVERY TIME
D★S

THIS REGAL PROFILE... HER ROYAL MAJESTY, CATHERINE L'PREMIERE.
SHE'S GORGEOUS!
EEEK!

BUT SHE IS NO ORDINARY CAT...
SHE SMELLS LIKE THAT "CALPIS" DRINK.

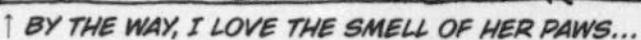
↑ BY THE WAY, I LOVE THE SMELL OF HER PAWS...

GROOM MY HAIR, MASTER.
SHE DOESN'T EVEN TRY TO GROOM HER OWN FUR LIKE A NORMAL CAT.

AND SOMETIMES SHE JUST HAS A BIG OL' TURD HANGING FROM IT! LIKE I SAID, NOT A NORMAL CAT!!

Until Death do us Part

Art Staff
Suri ♀: Chief Assistant
0-Second ♂: Background Art
Taurus ♀: Background Art

Military Advisor
Lee Hyun Seok (warmania)

SPECIAL THANKS
Shingo Takano

Crossover Planning
JESUS—Sajin Kouro, Yami no Aegis, Akatsuki no Aegis
Written by Kyouichi Nanatsuki, Art by Yoshihide Fujiwara
(Shogakukan)

Design Assistance
Hitoshi Fukuchi

chapter 171

YOU'RE SAYING THAT MUSASHI ONLY ENTERED FIGHTS HE KNEW HE WAS LIKELY TO WIN?
AT THE VERY LEAST, HE HAD A PROPER MEANS OF VICTORY FOR JUST ABOUT EVERY DUEL THAT WAS RECORDED.
THIS IS THE PREVAILING VIEW IN JAPAN TODAY, AND MY ANALYSIS BACKS IT UP.

HE WAS NOT THE MODEL OF THE "SAMURAI" MENTALITY.
AMONG HIS CONTEMPORARIES, HIS BATTLE TECHNIQUE WAS MUCH CLOSER TO WESTERN PRAGMATISM.
HE WAS A BRILLIANT MAN, FAR CLEVERER THAN ANYONE AROUND HIM.

IF YOU REALLY WANT A VIEW INTO THE WAY OF THE BUSHI, THE BEST MANUAL IS *HAGAKURE*.
MM.

I'M SURPRISED THAT SOMEONE FROM A DIFFERENT PART OF THE WORLD WOULD DELVE SO DEEPLY INTO BOTH *THE ART OF WAR* AND *THE BOOK OF FIVE RINGS*.

I'M AN AVID READER.

...

HOW'D THEY START TALKING ABOUT SOME ANCIENT SAMURAI BULLSHIT !?

HEY, SAMURAI!
GACHA (KCHUNK)

C'MON, I WANT A REMATCH!
SHU (FSS)
SHU

I'M NOT SATISFIED WITH THAT LAST ONE.
LET'S DO IT ONE-ON-ONE THIS TIME. I WASN'T ABLE TO EXECUTE MY FULL STYLE BEFORE.

IS YOUR FOOT ALL RIGHT?
THANKS TO THE FACT THAT YOU DIDN'T PIERCE THE BONE.

IF YOU CAN ACCURATELY AVOID AN OPPONENT'S MOVE WITHIN TWO INCHES...

...THEN ZELM CAN DO IT WITHIN HALF AN INCH.
!?
UNTIL YOU CAN REACH THAT LEVEL, YOU HAVE NO BUSINESS FACING ME OR AEGIS.
...
YES, EVERY MEMBER OF THE TRUMPS IS FIRST-RATE.
BUT THE ONLY OTHER MEMBER EVEN CLOSE TO BEING ULTRA-ELITE IS DEGA OVER THERE.
...FINE... MAYBE HE AIN'T SO DUMB AFTER ALL.

BUT ASIDE FROM GENIE, ZELM, N'SINH, AND WITH THE EXCEPTION OF THE SNIPER SHIEDABRA, NONE OF YOU STAND A CHANCE AGAINST ME.
BA (SPIN)
WHAT !?

I MAY HAVE LOST TO JESUS...
...BUT I DON'T REMEMBER LOSING TO YOU!!
YOU DON'T GET IT.
WHAT DO YOU MEAN!?

YOU HELD YOUR OWN AGAINST JESUS BECAUSE YOU WERE THE PERFECT MATCH AGAINST HIM.
!?
BUT THIS MAN IS YOUR WORST NIGHTMARE IN THAT REGARD. YOU WOULDN'T LAST A MINUTE!

Y-YOU DON'T KNOW THAT UNLESS WE FIGHT!!

YOU AND INVISIBLE...
...ARE ESPE-CIALLY POORLY SUITED TO FIGHT ME.

...

YOU'RE GONNA USE THAT AS A REASON TO DUCK OUT OF A FIGHT, SAMURAI?

WAIT YOUR TURN!
I'M FIRST, SAMURAI!

SHUT UP!!
KNOCK IT OFF WITH ALL THE "SAMURAI" CRAP!

SAMURAI IS ONLY FOR PEOPLE WHO WORK ADMIRABLY AND HONORABLY FOR THEIR IDEALS!!
I'M JUST A SWORDSMAN! CARRYING A KATANA AND SWINGING IT AROUND DOESN'T MAKE YOU A SAMURAI!! GOT THAT, FOREIGNERS !?

GACHA (KCHIK)
ガチャ

... MAMORU ...

THE FUCK'S HIS PROB-LEM!?

...

HEY, WHY ARE YOU SO UPTIGHT!?
IT'S NOT *LIKE* YOU.

I ENDED UP EXPLAINING A BUNCH OF BORING CRAP THAT NO ONE ASIDE FROM ZELM WOULD UNDERSTAND.
I NEED MORE DISCIPLINE.

ARE YOU IRRITATED ABOUT WHAT HAPPENED TO AGENT GENDA?
...

I'M RIGHT, AREN'T I?

I BEAR RESPONSI-BILITY—NO, NOT QUITE. I'M NOT SURE HOW TO SAY IT.
THE CONNECTION BETWEEN US THAT I CREATED CAUSED ME TO EVENTUALLY OWE HIM A DEBT.

IF I DON'T FREE HARUKA SOON, I'LL HAVE A HARD TIME SLEEPING, KNOWING THAT IT'S GONE UNPAID.

I SEE...A "SAMURAI," HUH...
I SUPPOSE YOU COULD SEE HIM AS A MANIFESTATION OF THAT VERY CODE.

IS THAT WHY YOU RUSHED THE PLAN?
EX-ACTLY.
ALL OF THIS SNEAKING, UNDERHANDED BULLSHIT FROM GROWN ADULTS FIGHTING OVER A SINGLE LITTLE GIRL...
I'M GOING TO PUT AN END TO IT FOR GOOD!!

I FEEL SORRY FOR WHAT TURUS GOT DRAGGED INTO.
HE'S THE ASSHOLE WHO CREATED THIS SITUATION IN THE FIRST PLACE.
A THOUSAND SLICES WOULDN'T BE ENOUGH FOR THE LIKES OF HIM.

SO THAT'S WHY HE DOESN'T JUST KILL THE GUY...

MAKES SENSE, I GUESS.

KO (TOKK)
ZELM?
DO YOU MIND SPARRING WITH THESE TWO FOR A BIT? WE'VE GOT IMPORTANT WORK LATER...
...AND I CAN'T HAVE THEM FLYING OFF THE HANDLE OVER THIS SQUABBLE WHEN IT COUNTS.

I SEE. YOU WANT TO SEPARATE THE MEN FROM THE BOYS.
WELL, OF COURSE YOU DO.
YOUR PUPILS MUST BE PRETTY STUPID IF THEY NEED TO LEARN THIS LESSON THE HARD WAY.

I MUST SADLY AGREE.

BUT AT LEAST THEY'RE DEDICATED AND STUB-BORN.
I LIKE GUYS LIKE THAT.

I CHOSE THEM FOR THOSE VERY QUALITIES.

Until Death do us Part

JAAA
(GRUNN)

chapter 172

ギュルルル
GYURURURU (VUUUN)
UGH...
HNNNG !!
ズザザザ
ZUZAZAZA (ZWUMM)

YOU'RE TAKING TOO LONG, IBUKI!!

DON'T ACT LIKE IT SHOULD BE EASY! THERE'S ALL KINDS OF PROBLEMS HERE!!
MY MACHINE'S BUILT FOR THE CITY! NOBODY RETUNES A BIKE LIKE THAT TO PLAY IN THE MUD!!

COULDN'T YOU JUST USE SPARC?
THE BOSS LET US USE HIM WITHOUT RESERVATION.
WELL, HE AIN'T HUMAN, SO HE DOESN'T UNDERSTAND THE FINER DETAILS.

HE'S NOT BUILT TO FINE-TUNE AN INTERFACE THAT ACTUAL HUMAN BEINGS USE!

IF YOU JUST TOLD HIM WHICH NUMBERS TO USE, I'M SURE IT WOULD WORK JUST FINE.
BUT IBUKI DOES THINGS BY FEEL, SO HE WOULDN'T KNOW THEM...

BUT EVEN OUTSIDE OF IDEAL CONDITIONS, HIJIKATA NEVER MADE EXCUSES.

UGH...
...

Y-YOU WANT TO ME TO DO IT? FINE!!
...

JUST WAIT...I'LL BLOW YOUR MIND!!
ギュイイイ
GYUIII (GREEE)

キュルルル
GYURURURU (GLURRRK)

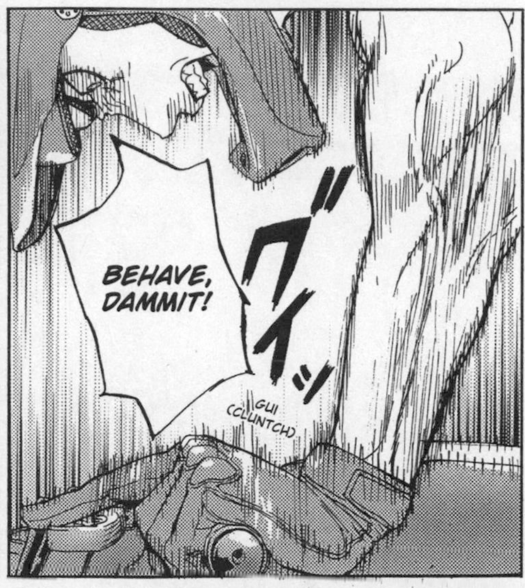
BEHAVE, DAMMIT!
GUI (CLUNTCH)

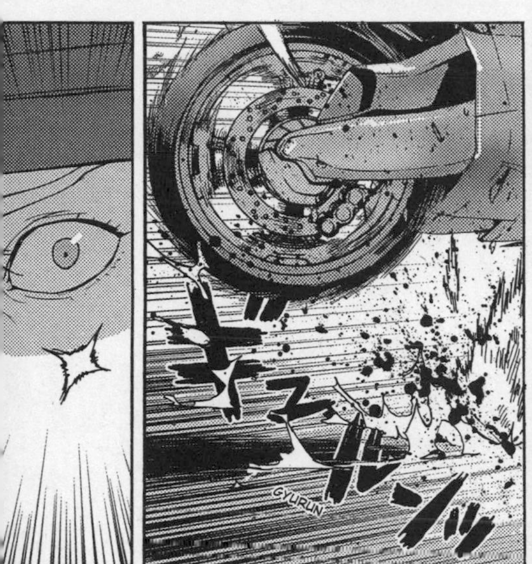
GYURUN

GA (WHAM)
GA
GA
GA

NYAARGH!!
WHAT KIND OF ARM STRENGTH IS THAT?
HE CLEARED THE COURSE ON WILL-POWER ALONE...
HE'S A GENIUS, NO DOUBT ABOUT IT.
RAAAAH!!
ゴッ
GO (WHUD)

GULP!

AAAAAHHHH!
SADLY... HE'S ALSO AN *IDIOT*.

...I SUPPOSE GENIUS AND IDIOCY CAN CO-EXIST...

DAMN ...

The operation will begin at the northern border.

SPARC
speaking
Unlike with Galboa, Duhana's border security is a sieve—the black market needs foreigners to be able to visit without trouble.

EXACTLY. IT'S A COUNTRY OF EXTREME POVERTY AND OPPRESSION.
IT SOUNDS LIKE A HORRIBLE PLACE...
FOR IMMIGRANTS AND REFUGEES, THERE'S NOTHING TO BE GAINED BY GOING TO DUHANA.
ON THE OTHER HAND, THEY HAVE FULLY-MANNED FORCES TO KEEP THEIR OWN PEOPLE FROM LEAVING. BE WARY OF THEM.
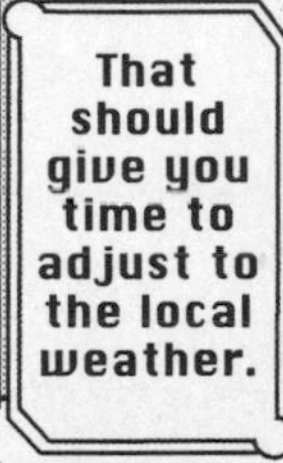

The team will be on location to prepare a week before Mamoru Hijikata is scheduled to arrive.
SPARC speaking
ピッ
PI (PING)
That should give you time to adjust to the local weather.

You will make use of satellite-aided navigation tools to follow the targets.
Our battle-tested units, Shot, Juliet, and Elan will be stationed at the site. Dai Ibuki and Pyro will be commandos.

...
Senji-san will stay in the command vehicle with me to protect the base of operations.
ROGER!
SPARC speaking

COM-MANDER, TO BE HONEST, WE'RE LOW ON SUPPORT AT PRESENT.
I'D LIKE TO REQUEST MORE MEMBERS JUST TO BE SAFE.
WHAT ROLES WOULD THEY PLAY?
Miss Haruka, we have received a recommen-dation on the topic of reinforce-ments.
WHO?
SPARC speaking

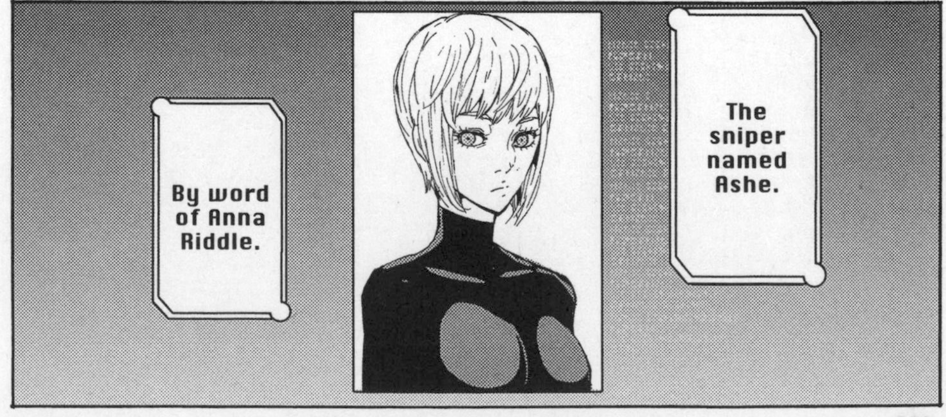
The sniper named Ashe.
By word of Anna Riddle.

I will look into the matter.
ASHE-SAN!?
キキッ
KIKI (SCREECH)
Elan has arrived.

ザッ
ZA (ZSH)
ガチャッ
SACHA (CLICK)

FORGIVE ME FOR ARRIVING LATE. I'M HERE TO JOIN THE TEAM.

SIERRA-SAN!?
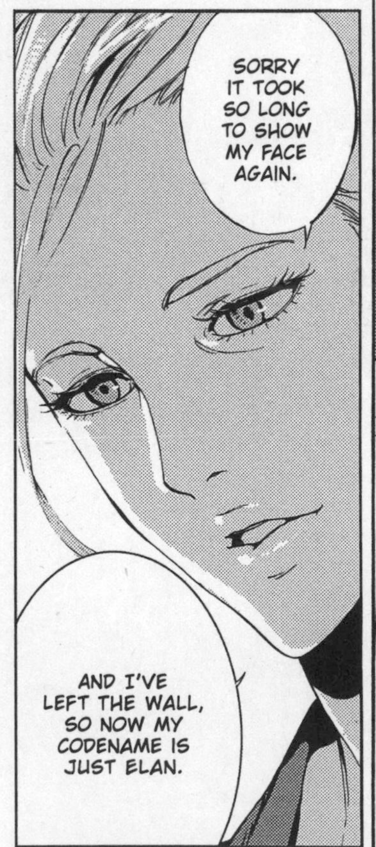
SORRY IT TOOK SO LONG TO SHOW MY FACE AGAIN.
AND I'VE LEFT THE WALL, SO NOW MY CODENAME IS JUST ELAN.

!?
INABA-SENSEI ...???
IT'S BEEN A WHILE!
SENJI !?

EEEP!
I-I-INABA-SENSEI!
YOU KNOW EACH OTHER?
HE WAS A TERRIBLE FORMER DISCIPLE OF MINE!

SENJI-SAN WAS?
BACK IN HOKKAIDO, THEY SAID THAT TESSHUU INABA-SENSEI WAS AN UNBEATABLE SWORDSMAN, A MODERN-DAY MUSASHI.
AND I WAS LURED BY THOSE STORIES INTO JOINING HIS SCHOOL...

HMM, ODD STORY... I'VE NEVER HEARD THAT ONE BEFORE...
REALLY!?
HE HAD PROMISE AS A PUPIL.
SPENT THREE YEARS WITH US IN S TEENS, EN JUST APPEARED THOUT A RACE ONE DAY.

TEST IT.
AFTER THAT, I SELF-STUDIED ...
DOESN'T THAT MEAN YOU WERE MAMORU-SAN'S SENIOR AS APPRENTICES!?
NO WAY, NO HOW! I COULDN'T POSSIBLY EMBARRASS MYSELF BY CLAIMING SENIORITY OVER A MASTER LIKE HIM!

OF COURSE YOU CAN'T! I EXPELLED YOU FROM THE SCHOOL AGES AGO!!
N-NAT-URALLY, SENSEI!
AND YOU WOUND UP A YAKUZA OF ALL THINGS! IT'S AN EMBARRASS-MENT!

...
I CAME TO TOKYO TO PAY MY RESPECTS TO GENDA.

FRANKLY, THERE'S NO WAY SHE CAN MATCH MAMORU AFTER JUST A FEW MONTHS OF TRAINING...
...BUT I FIGURED I WOULD SPENT EVERY LAST MOMENT I COULD TEACHING HER.

!?

THERE ARE MANY THINGS YOU CAN'T LEARN UNLESS YOU FORGET WHAT YOU'VE ALREADY BUILT UP.
SHE'S GOT THE BASICS DRUMMED INTO HER, BUT SHE LACKS THE REFINEMENT OF EXPERIENCE.

I'D BE HAPPY JUST HAVING ENOUGH SKILL TO PROTECT YOU...
...BUT SENSEI SAYS THAT'S NOT ENOUGH.

OF COURSE NOT!
I CAN'T TOSS A PUPIL OUT INTO THE WILD TO DIE!

PARDON ME.
DO YOU THINK YOU COULD GIVE ME SOME LESSONS TOO!?

I WISH TO DO MY PROPER DUTY TO THE YOUNG MISS AS A BULLET SPONGE!!

VERY WELL.
IT WAS GENDA WHO BROUGHT US HERE. I MIGHT AS WELL CARE FOR ALL OF YOU.

THANK YOU, SIR.

NOW...
...WHAT COMES NEXT WILL BE A BIT ROUGH.

PREPARE YOUR-SELVES.

...

TH...
THANK YOU, SIR.

YOU'VE GROWN SO BIG AND BRAVE...

?
I HAVE? I CAN'T TELL.

YES, YOU HAVE... BUT WEREN'T YOU STARTLED WHEN I ARRIVED?
I WAS.

THAT'S A BAD SIGN. DON'T GET TOO STRESSED OUT RIGHT NOW, OR YOU'LL NEVER LAST UNTIL THE BIG OPERATION.
HUH?
OKAY, I'LL TRY MY BEST!

...

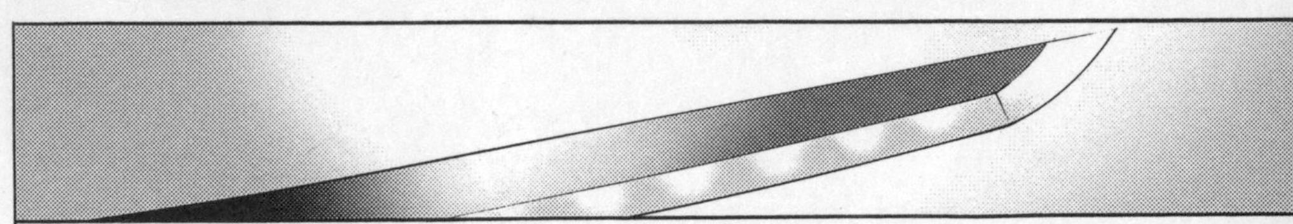

Until Death do us Part

chapter 173

JUST WAIT...I'LL SEND YOU SPRAWLING THIS TIME...

THAT'S THREE LOSSES IN A ROW FOR YOU...
I ADMIRE YOUR DEDICATION...
SHUT UP!!

BUO
(VWOOM)
HYU
(SWISH)
TAN
(TOMP)
!?
GYURU
(SPIN)

HYUN

PASHI (SNATCH)

I SEE. YOU BOUNCED IT OFF THE CORNER OF THE CONTAINER ...
...CAUSING THE WEIGHT TO COUNTER-SPIN AND TAKE AN UNEXPECTED HOP.

BUT TRICKS LIKE THAT WON'T HELP YOU ERASE YOUR WEAPON'S FLAWS.

HMPH! SAVE YOUR CROWING FOR WHEN YOU'VE WON!!
BUO (WHOOSH)
CHECK THIS OUT!!

ANOTHER BALL IN THE SAME SPOT!?

KIN
(TING)

ZA
(ZSSH)
UGH!

THAT ONE ACTUALLY MADE ME SWEAT, BUT IF YOU'D COME UP WITH THAT LITTLE TRICK A BIT EARLIER, YOU MIGHT'VE SHOWN JESUS A THING OR TWO.

...

YOU'VE MADE GREAT PROGRESS OVER THESE THREE FIGHTS.
JUST NOT NEARLY ENOUGH TO MAKE UP FOR YOUR DISADVANTAGE.

NEXT UP IS ME.
KAN
KAN (CLACK)

THESE FLIES ARE BUGGING ME.
TAKE 'EM OUT WITH YOUR SPECIAL PUNCH.

BO (VOOM)
HEH!

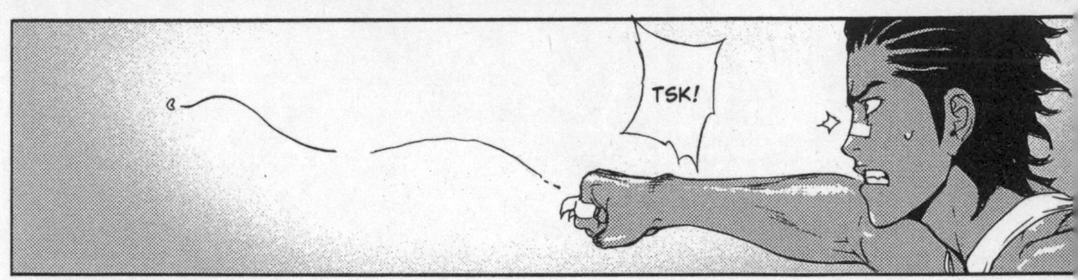
TSK!

IF YOU WANT TO DROP A FLY, YOU EITHER HAVE TO PUNCH FASTER OR AIM WITH THE KNUCKLE SPIKES.

YOU GOTTA BE CRAZY! YOU CAN'T AIM AT A TINY THING LIKE THAT!

HMPH!
HYU (SWISH)

KASA (SKITTER)
カサ
KASA
カサ

...YOU'RE RIGHT. IT'S IMPOS-SIBLE...
WHA—!?

A FLY CAN TURN 90 DEGREES IN JUST 30 MILLI-SECONDS.
HUMAN REFLEXES ARE PHYSICALLY INCAPABLE OF KNOCKING ONE OUT OF THE AIR.

HUH ???

IN FACT, HUMAN REFLEXES ARE SLOWER THAN MOST ANIMALS' AND INSECTS'.
BUT THERE'S A FAMOUS CLAIM THAT THE GREAT MIYAMOTO MUSASHI GRABBED A FLY OUT OF THE AIR WITH HIS CHOP-STICKS. HOW DO YOU SUPPOSE HE DID THAT?

HUH!? UM, BY...

RIGHT. BY THINKING.

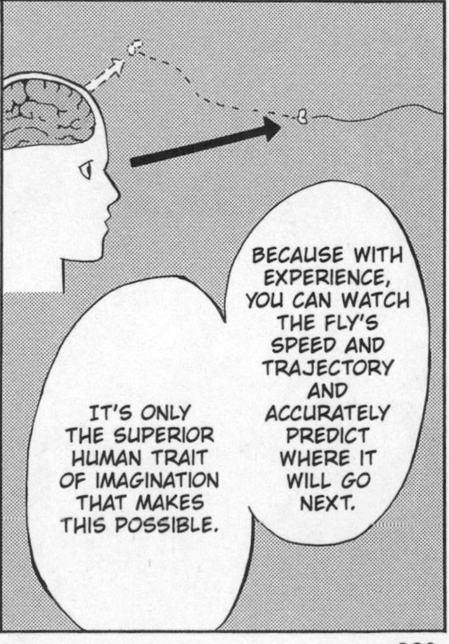
BECAUSE WITH EXPERIENCE, YOU CAN WATCH THE FLY'S SPEED AND TRAJECTORY AND ACCURATELY PREDICT WHERE IT WILL GO NEXT.
IT'S ONLY THE SUPERIOR HUMAN TRAIT OF IMAGINATION THAT MAKES THIS POSSIBLE.

YOU BEAT A LION TO DEATH, DIDN'T YOU?
YOU BEAT THE LION'S REACTION SPEED. THERE'S NO REASON YOU COULDN'T ACHIEVE THAT.

NOW LET'S BEGIN.

WHO SAID THEY COULD HAVE FUN DOWN THERE?

AFTER ALL THE BOASTING, THEY'RE GETTING ALONG JUST FINE.
THE OLD BADGER.

THIS IS AUGMENTING THE GROUP'S STRENGTH.
HM?

HMM.
AND MAMORU HIJIKATA IS GOING ALONG WITH IT. HE KNOWS WHAT'S HAPPENING.
THE MORE EXPERIENCED THE TEAM, THE SMOOTHER THE PLAN WILL GO.
THAT WAS PART OF ZELM'S IDEA.

YET YOU ARE OBSERVING THE EXERCISE.
HE'S SUR-PRISINGLY SKILLED AT TEACHING.
DOESN'T MEAN ANYTHING TO A SNIPER LIKE ME.

WHETHER YOU REALIZE IT OR NOT, YOU'RE ALL PARTICIPATING.

AND SO IS HE.

...YOU'RE PLENTY CRAFTY YOURSELF.

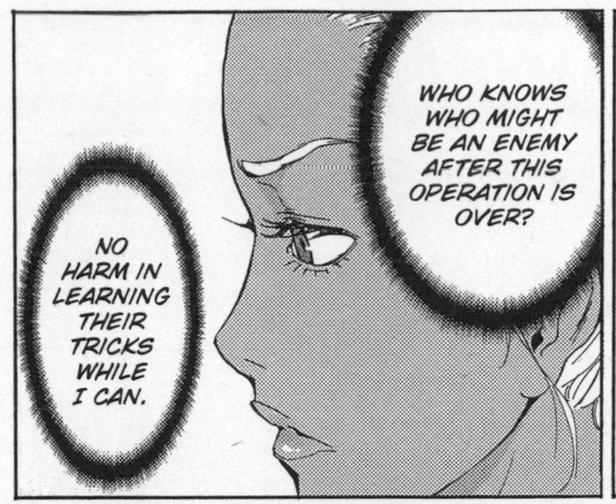
WHO KNOWS WHO MIGHT BE AN ENEMY AFTER THIS OPERATION IS OVER?
NO HARM IN LEARNING THEIR TRICKS WHILE I CAN.

ZUSHAAA (ZSSHH)

SHIT!!
GON (THUD)

WHY WON'T IT WORK!?

BECAUSE YOU ALL HAVE A FUNDAMENTAL MISUNDER-STANDING OF THE KATANA.

WHAT DO YOU MEAN?

THINK OF WHEN IT WAS DEVELOPED, FOOL.
BACK IN THE SENGOKU ERA, IF YOU SURVIVED THE FLINTLOCKS AND BOWS, THE PRIMARY WEAPONS WERE POLEARMS LIKE SPEARS AND NAGINATAS!

ORIGINALLY, THIS WAS DESIGNED FOR SELF-DEFENSE.
IT'S LIKE A PISTOL IN MODERN TERMS—A SIDEARM.
A GIANT SWORD LIKE THAT?

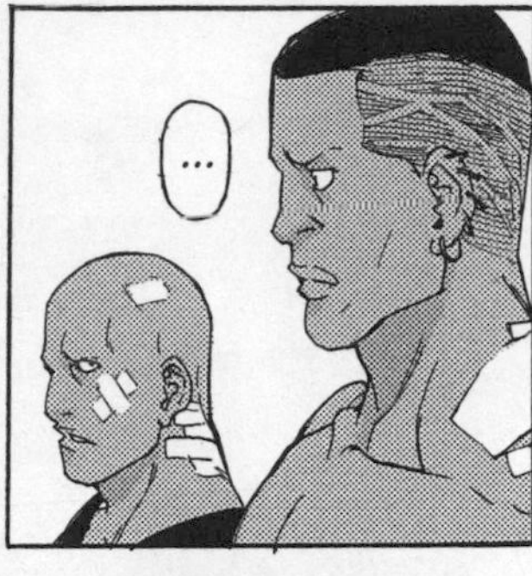
...

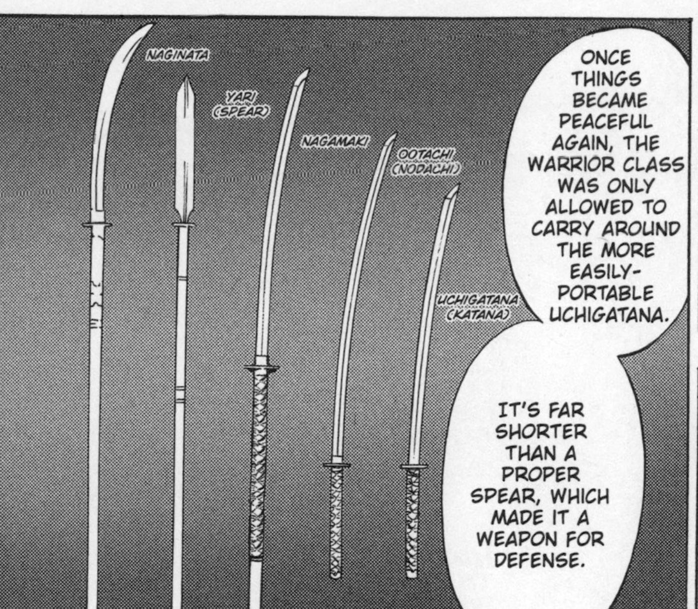
NAGINATA
YARI (SPEAR)
NAGAMAKI
OOTACHI (NODACHI)
UCHIGATANA (KATANA)
ONCE THINGS BECAME PEACEFUL AGAIN, THE WARRIOR CLASS WAS ONLY ALLOWED TO CARRY AROUND THE MORE EASILY-PORTABLE UCHIGATANA.
IT'S FAR SHORTER THAN A PROPER SPEAR, WHICH MADE IT A WEAPON FOR DEFENSE.

PUT A NAGAMAKI IN MY HANDS...
...AND I'LL HAVE FIVE TIMES THE DESTRUCTIVE POWER.

THE TRUE VALUE OF A KATANA IS ITS ABILITY TO DEFEND.
IF YOU CHALLENGE SOMEONE WITH A TOOL LIKE THAT, IT NATURALLY CHANGES HOW YOU APPROACH THEM, DOESN'T IT?

...
...I SEE...

THEN WHY DO YOU FIGHT WITH THAT THING!?
WHY NOT JUST USE A DAMN SPEAR!?

BECAUSE *THIS* IS WHAT I'M BEST SUITED TO SWING.
THE ONLY TIME I COMPROMISED ON THAT WAS WHEN I USED THE LONG NODACHI AGAINST ZELM.

...HEH...
SAMURAI'S HOLDING THE REINS NOW.

BUT THAT'S ALL FINE AND GOOD. FIGHTING THE STRONG WILL MAKE YOU STRONGER.
NEXT!!

I CAN'T RETURN TO GALBOA LIKE THIS ...
...WITHOUT HAVING AVENGED MY SHAME ...

DAD WILL KILL ME...

The man who rules over the quasi-state of Duhana is Colonel Zashid Turus.
SPARC speaking
His precise age is unclear, but estimates put it between 35 and 50.
All around Africa, he is known as "Mr. Darkside."
SPARC speaking
He belongs to a local tribe ethnically, but his ancestors mixed blood over and over...
...to the point that his own ethnic makeup is impossible to categorize.
In recognition of this, he wears a striking tattoo pattern that integrates his back-ground into his physical features.
This is the only available footage of him.

1.00x
1:15:28/2:02:09

!?

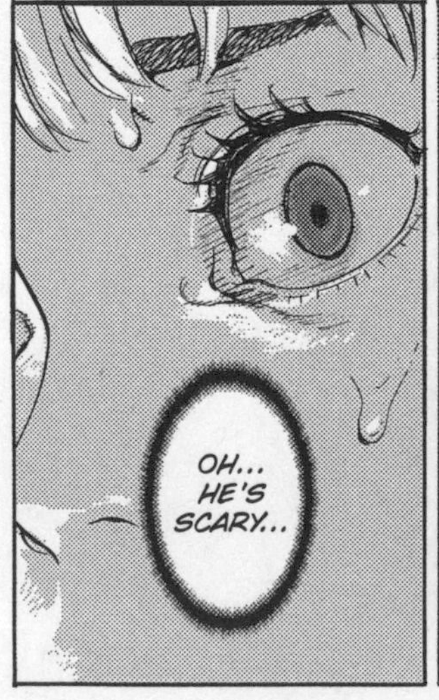
OH... HE'S SCARY...

WE CAN'T! NOBODY CAN MATCH HIM...NOT EVEN MAMORU-SAN...
I CAN'T LET THE TWO OF THEM MEET!!

CAPITAL OF DUHANA, ZOTT

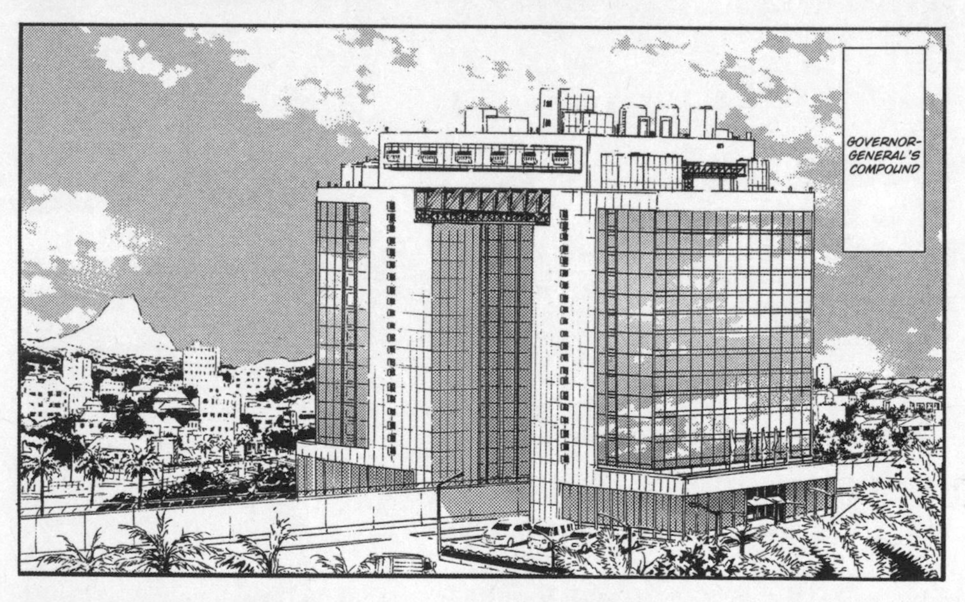
GOVERNOR-GENERAL'S COMPOUND

HMPH. AN AUDIENCE?
I'M IN NO MOOD TO MEET WITH THESE UNDERLINGS.
BUT, COLONEL ...
THEY OUGHT TO STAY QUIET AND PRODUCE HUMANS LIKE THEY'RE SUPPOSED TO.
MR. DARKSIDE.
YOU CAN'T JUST IGNORE US OUT OF HAND. WE'RE YOUR BUSINESS PARTNERS.
WE OUGHT TO BE ON EQUAL FOOTING.
...

chapter 174

Until Death do us Part

ARE YOU LISTENING TO ME, COLONEL?
TEN PERCENT OF THE ENORMOUS WEALTH OUR FACTORY PRODUCES GOES INTO YOUR POCKET.

THIS IS AN UNTHINKABLE CONCESSION FROM THE TPC'S PER-SPECTIVE.
NORMALLY, EVEN THREE PERCENT IS CONSIDERED HIGH.

SILENCE.

IT'S A FORTUNE THAT ANY RURAL DESPOT WOULD KILL TO GET HIS HANDS ON.
BUT INSTEAD OF THANKING US, YOU TURN US AWAY AT THE DOOR? THAT'S JUST—

SILENCE.

HYU
(SWISH)
???

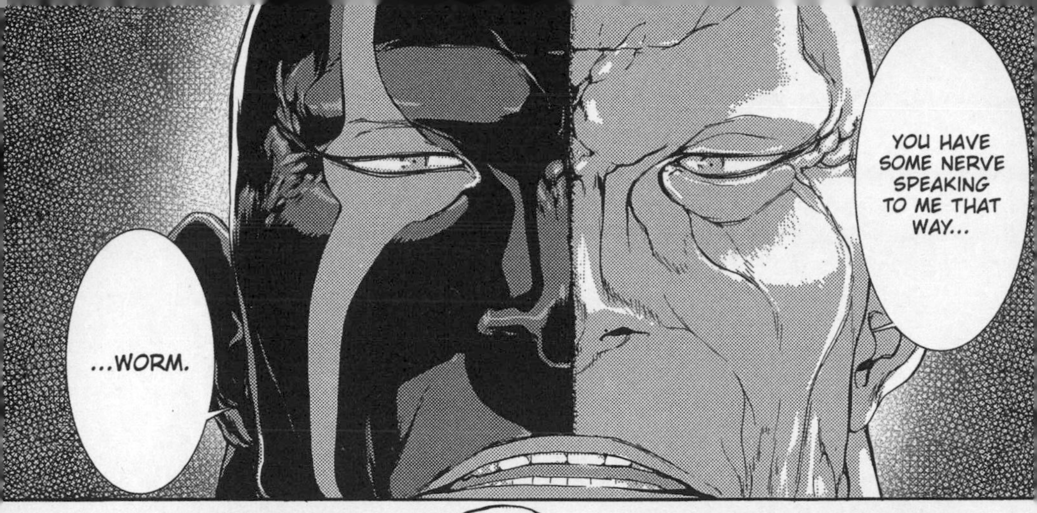
YOU HAVE SOME NERVE SPEAKING TO ME THAT WAY...
...WORM.

AH...
AAAH!
YOU HAVE RUINED MY PRECIOUS QUIET TIME WITH YOUR SCREECHING VOICE.

YOUR LIFE IS NOT WORTH EVEN MY PINKY FINGER.
ピッ
PI
ピッ
PI
ピッ
PI (RIP)
GULP.

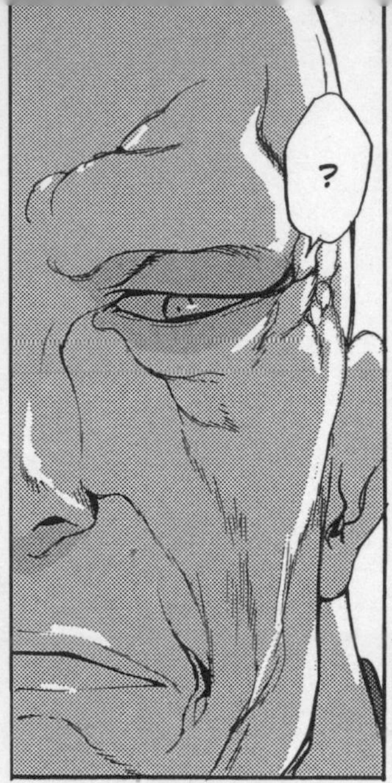
?

... JESÚS IS ACTIVE NOW...

JESUS, SWORN ENEMY OF THE TPC, HAS ENTERED ZIMBABWE.
WE BELIEVE HE SEEKS TO DESTROY OUR FACTORY.

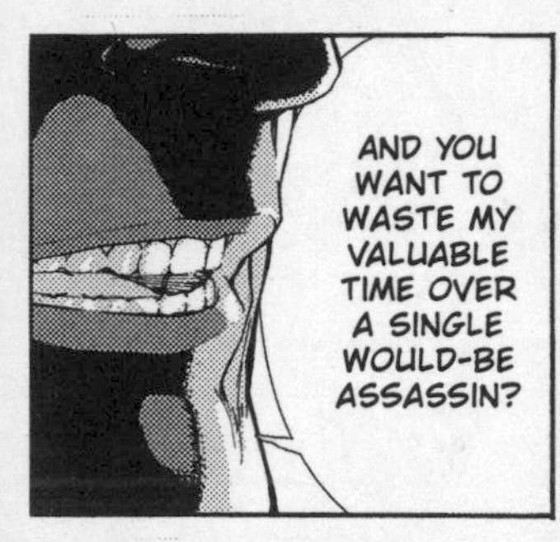
AND YOU WANT TO WASTE MY VALUABLE TIME OVER A SINGLE WOULD-BE ASSASSIN?

IF HE IS NOT STOPPED, YOU WILL BE HELD RESPONSIBLE FOR HIM...

ピピピッ
PIPIPI
(RRRIP)

NNN!

スッ
SU
(SHH)

YOUR DEDICATION TO YOUR WORK HAS EARNED YOU A REPRIEVE.

AHHH!
BUT REMEMBER THIS.

IN THIS COUNTRY, MY ORDERS ARE ABSOLUTE.
YOU WILL NOT DEFY MY WILL A SECOND TIME.
MAJOR!
SIR.
SEND THE GIDO BATTERY TO THE FACTORY. ASSIGN A HEAD OF SECURITY.
ANYONE WHO APPROACHES THE FACTORY WITHOUT AUTHORIZATION IS TO BE KILLED.
SIR!

I WILL DISPATCH ONE OF MY SONS. ANY COMPLAINTS!?
O-OF COURSE NOT.
YOUR SONS ARE KNOWN FAR AND WIDE AS THE FIERCEST AND BRAVEST WARRIORS AROUND.

HMPH... THEY'RE IDIOTS, EACH AND EVERY ONE.
OH !?

ENOUGH. BEGONE.
YES, SIR!
ギィ...
GII... (CREAK)

AHHH
...

YOU DID GOOD TO HOLD IT IN.
HUH?
IF YOU'D GIVEN IN TO THE FEAR OF FALLING AND GRABBED ONTO HIM, HE WOULD'VE RIPPED YOUR WRIST RIGHT OUT OF THE FOREARM.

YOU'RE LUCKY. HE LIKES YOU MORE THAN THE OTHERS.

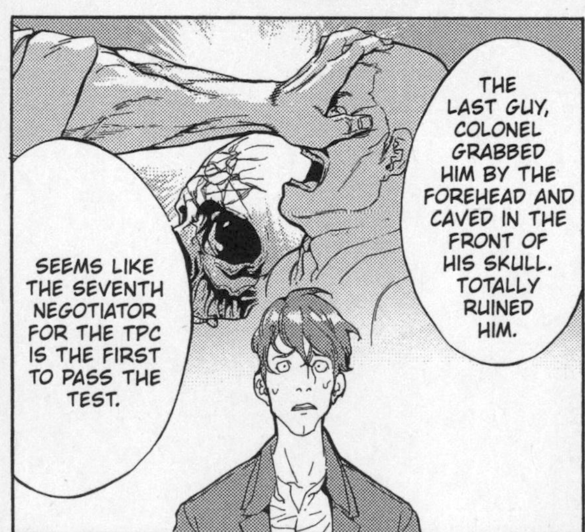
THE LAST GUY, COLONEL GRABBED HIM BY THE FOREHEAD AND CAVED IN THE FRONT OF HIS SKULL. TOTALLY RUINED HIM.
SEEMS LIKE THE SEVENTH NEGOTIATOR FOR THE TPC IS THE FIRST TO PASS THE TEST.

WHAT ABOUT... THE OTHER FIVE...?
クル
KURU (SPIN)
...

FED TO THE TIGERS, SHOT OUT OF CANNONS ...
ACTUALLY, YOU DON'T WANT TO HEAR ANY MORE THAN THAT.

UH...
......

Are you aware of Tosa fighting dogs?
YES, BUT I'VE NEVER ACTUALLY SEEN ONE FIGHT.

It's a cross between the Tosa breed from Shikoku and other breeds like Maeda, Mastiff, Bulldog, Pitbull, Great Dane, and others.
A man-made breed kept for fighting.
Zashid Turus is a member of an ethnic group bred for combat dating back to the slave trade of the Middle Ages.
He is descended from those people, all these years later.

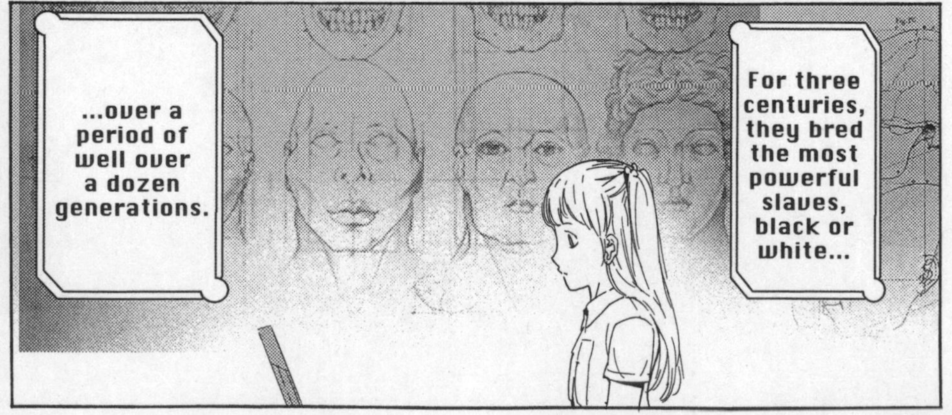
For three centuries, they bred the most powerful slaves, black or white...
...over a period of well over a dozen generations.

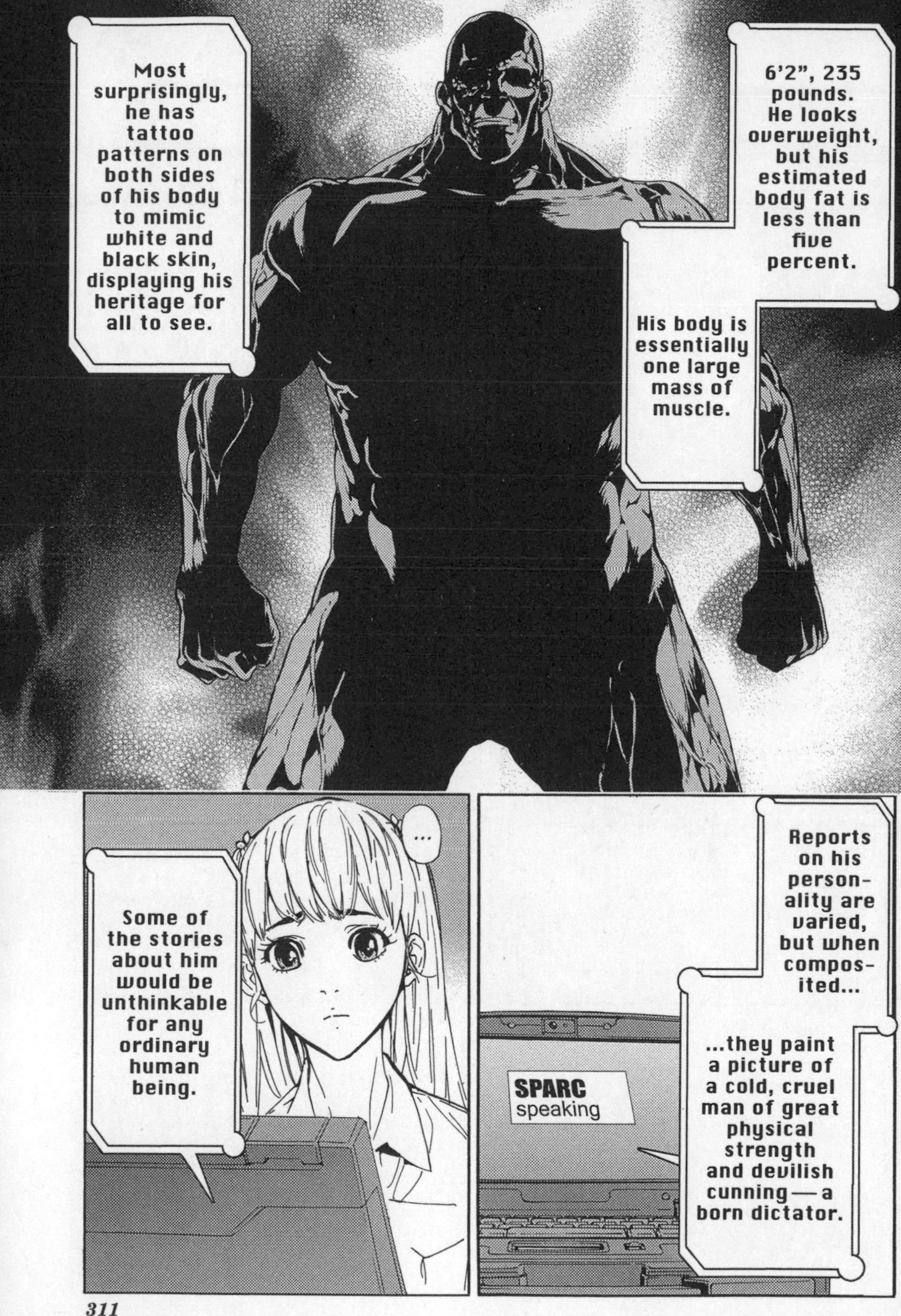

6'2", 235 pounds. He looks overweight, but his estimated body fat is less than five percent.
His body is essentially one large mass of muscle.
Most surprisingly, he has tattoo patterns on both sides of his body to mimic white and black skin, displaying his heritage for all to see.
Reports on his personality are varied, but when composited...
...they paint a picture of a cold, cruel man of great physical strength and devilish cunning—a born dictator.
SPARC speaking
...
Some of the stories about him would be unthinkable for any ordinary human being.

What's truly frightening is that despite this dreadful power, he is considered a hero of both Galboa and Duhana.
He splits popularity with President Ricardo Heitzman of Galboa, the public face of the government.

Their commitment to "might makes right" has taken tiny Galboa to U.N. membership, thanks to their military power.
The more advanced countries detest the man, but to the citizens, he is a hero who protected their land from colonial rule.
He's an effective leader.

Public support of the government is over eighty percent, at least among those with the right to vote.
This is in large part thanks to him.

MY DUTY IS TO SUBDUE MAMORU-SAN AND BRING HIM SAFELY BACK TO JAPAN!

I MUSTN'T LET MAMORU-SAN CONTACT COL. ZASHID TURUS!!

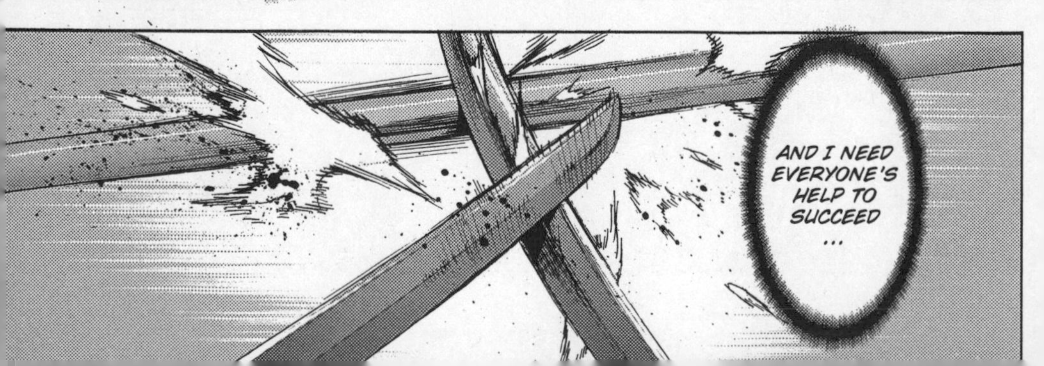
AND I NEED EVERYONE'S HELP TO SUCCEED ...

GA
(WHAK)
GA
GA

GA

GA
GA
GA

シャアアア
SHAAA (FSHHH)
シャアアア
SHAAA

GUY COULD USE SOME DISCIPLINE...

I WOULDN'T JUDGE HIM BASED ON HIS APPEARANCE.

WHAT DO YOU MEAN?
GU (HRP)

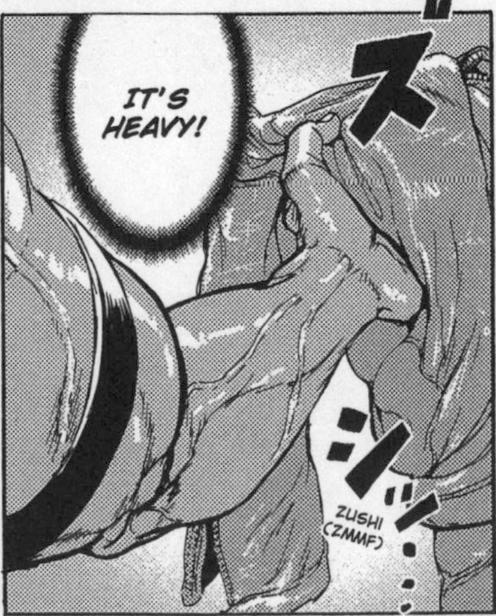
IT'S HEAVY!
ZUSHI (ZMMF)

BETWEEN THE ELECTRONICS AND THE SHOCK-ABSORBING GEL, THAT SUIT ALONE WEIGHS 125 POUNDS.
MOST PEOPLE CAN BARELY MOVE WEARING SOMETHING LIKE THAT.

THAT'S THE ONLY WAY TO STOP AN ASSAULT RIFLE BULLET WHILE ON A MOTOR-CYCLE, AND YOU WOULDN'T EXPECT ANYONE TO BE QUICK IN THE SADDLE.
BUT THE IDIOT HAS THE STAMINA AND TECHNIQUE TO PULL IT OFF WITH EASE. IT'S WHY HE WAS GRANTED USE OF BUCEPHALUS.
GOTCHA...
YOU NEED SKILL LIKE THAT TO SURVIVE THE JOB WE'RE ABOUT TO DO.

AFTER ALL, THIS WILL REQUIRE THE INTENT TO START A WAR WITH A SOVEREIGN NATION.

I'D LIKE TO AVOID THAT, IF POSSIBLE.
AND WHAT ABOUT YOU?
YOU SHOULD KNOW WHAT A THREAT DUHANA POSES, SHOULDN'T YOU?

YEAH. I WAS ONCE A MEMBER OF THE BLACK UNIT.
HUH!?

I DON'T SEE ANY REASON TO HIDE IT. I FLED THE COUNTRY WHEN DUHANA SPLIT OFF.
IT'S PART OF WHY I WAS CHOSEN FOR THIS OPERATION.

THAT'S REAS-SUR-ING TO KNOW.
SO YOU'VE GOT YOUR OWN STORY, JUST LIKE EVERYONE ELSE...

NARITA INTL. AIRPORT
Narita Airport Terminal 1

BECAUSE THERE ARE FEW DIRECT FLIGHTS TO MOZAMBIQUE AND OUR LOCAL EQUIPMENT AND FACILITIES NEEDED PREPARATION ...
...DAI-SAN'S GROUP LEFT BEFORE THE REST OF US.

WE WENT OVER OUR PREDICTIONS WITH A FINE-TOOTHED COMB UNTIL THE VERY LAST MOMENT...
...BUT ULTIMATELY, MAMORU-SAN AND WISEMAN'S PLAN WAS INDECIPHER-ABLE, AND I COULDN'T FORESEE ANYTHING BUT THE VAGUEST NOTIONS.

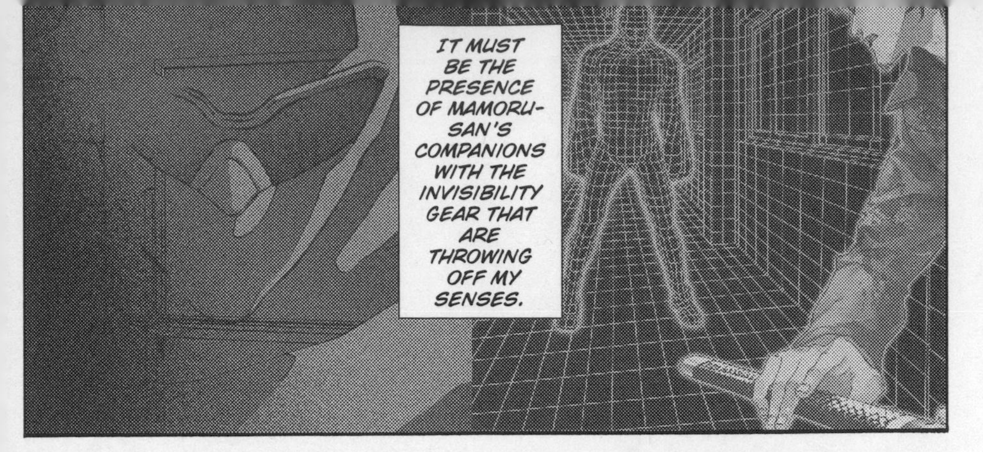
IT MUST BE THE PRESENCE OF MAMORU-SAN'S COMPANIONS WITH THE INVISIBILITY GEAR THAT ARE THROWING OFF MY SENSES.

出発(北口)

YOU SURE I DON'T NEED TO GO?
YOU HAVE A DUTY TO CAPTURE THE MEN WHO ATTACKED THE BUSINESS AND KILLED AGENT GENDA.
SHE WILL CATCH UP TO MAMORU HIJIKATA.

WAS IT HER PROPHETIC FORESIGHT?
HOW CAN YOU TELL?
...

JUST FEMALE INTUITION.
AHA
JA8
AHA

Until Death do us Part

chapter 175

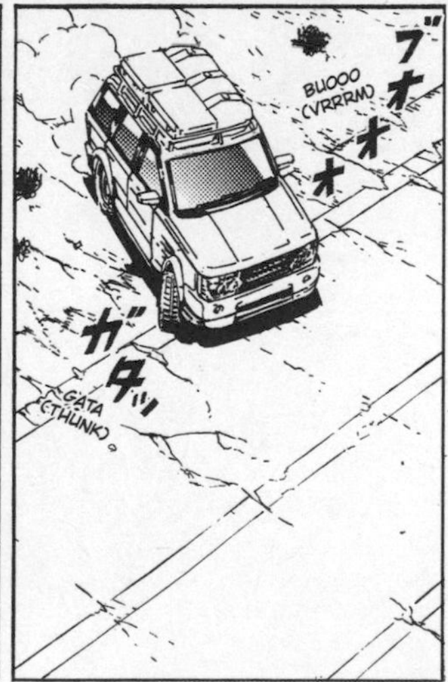
ブオオオ
BUOOO (VRRRM)
ガタッ
GATA (THUNK)

SO YOU FINALLY SHOWED UP.

...

YOU DON'T NEED ANY?

I KEEP MINE ON ME AT ALL TIMES.
OH... FINE.

OUR PREP-ARATIONS ARE 99% COMPLETE.
THE REST IS UP TO YOU. WE CAN CROSS THE BORDER AT ANY TIME.

IF YOU HAVE ANY WARNINGS OR CONCERNS, I'D LIKE TO HEAR THEM.

DUHANA DOESN'T HAVE A REAL AIR FORCE, BUT I'D STILL RECOMMEND NOT INVADING DURING THE DAY.
THEY DO HAVE SOMETHING OF A LAND PRESENCE ALONG THE BORDER.

THIS PLANE BELONGS TO A SMUGGLER WHO TRADES IN DUHANA.
THE CRAFT ITSELF WON'T COME UNDER SUSPICION, BUT THAT DOESN'T HOLD TRUE FOR ALL OF US.

I'D RECOM-MEND LEAVING AT A TIME OF DAY WHERE WE WON'T BE SPOTTED FROM THE GROUND.
...

THEN LET'S LEAVE IN THE MIDDLE OF THE NIGHT. I'LL LET YOU DECIDE THE BEST HOUR.
UNDER-STOOD.

WHERE SHOULD I PUT THESE DOWN?
OH, OVER THERE. WHER-EVER.

...

ゴオオオオ
GOHHH (VMMMMM)

ウイイーン
UIIIN (VREEE)

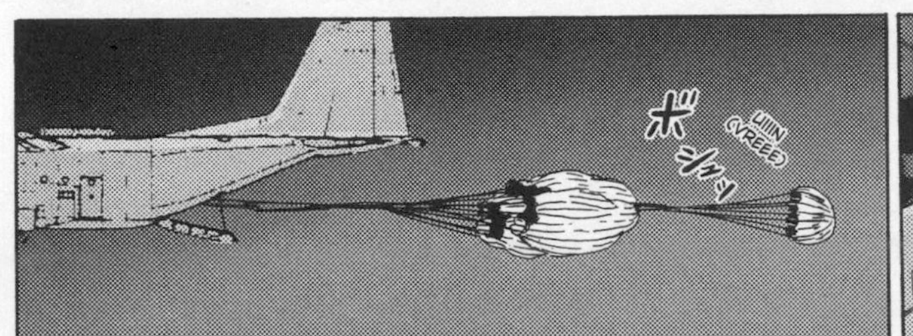
ボシュッ
BOSHU (SHUMP)

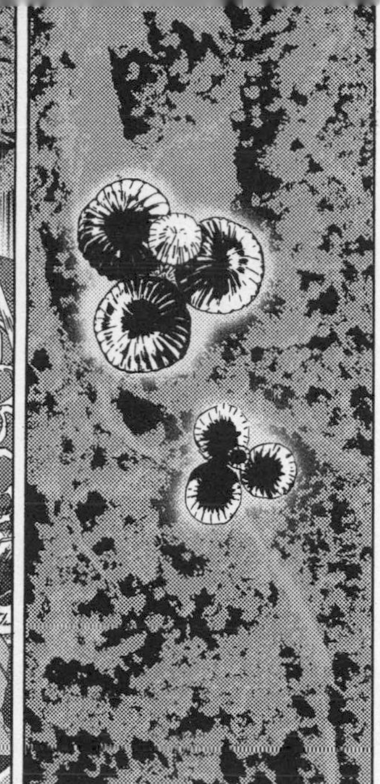

BASHAA
(SPLASH)

JACKPOT!

ZABAA
(ZZSHH)

BA
(VRRM)
BA
BA
BA

I've spotted them.
SPARC speaking

IF OUR SATELLITE IMAGES WERE ACCURATE, THIS SHOULD BE THE PLACE...

ALL ACCORDING TO PLAN?
RIGHT.

KOKU (NOD)
...

BAN (BOOM)
BEGIN SUPPRES-SION!!

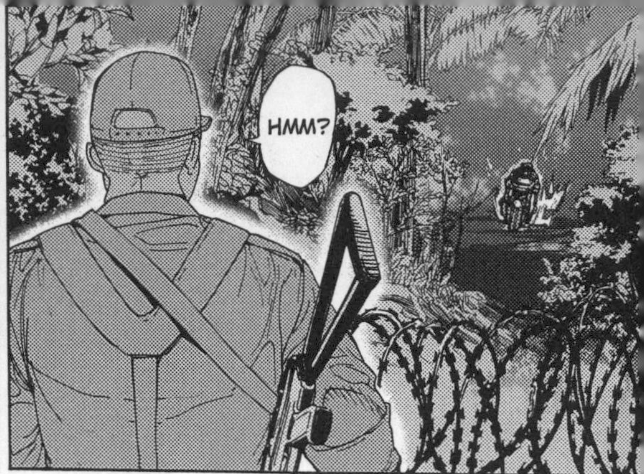
HMM?

CHA
(CHK)
チャ

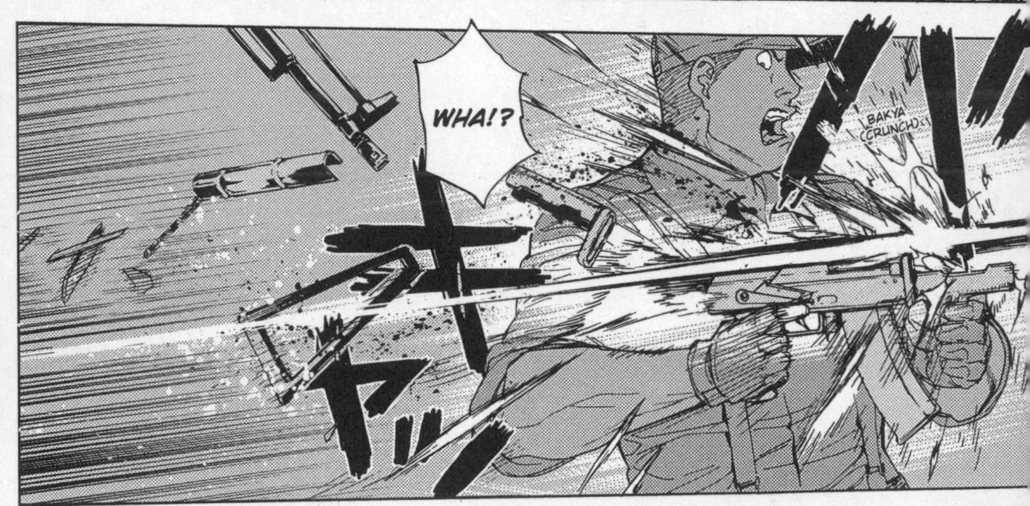
WHA!?
BAKYA
(CRUNCH)

KON
(TING)
コーン

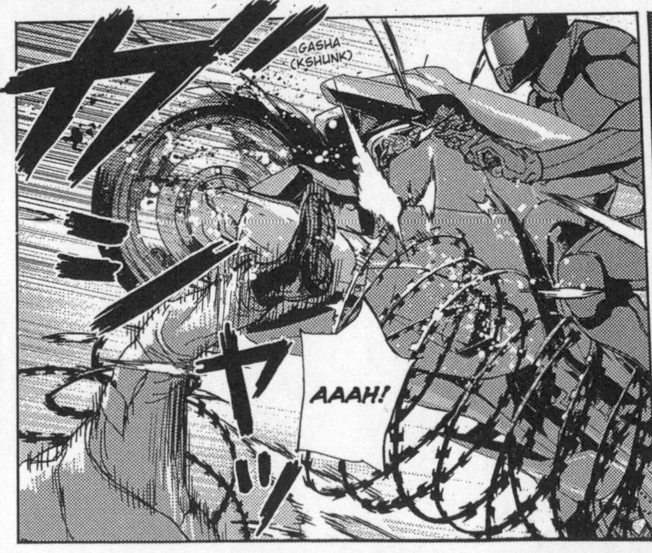
GASHA
(KSHUNK)
AAAH!

TA
(DASH)
TA
BASU
(FLIP)
WH-
WHAT'S
THAT!?
GYURURU
(SCREEE)
WHA
—!?
EEP!
WHAT'S
GOING
ON!?

SASA (SWISH)

AND NOW...

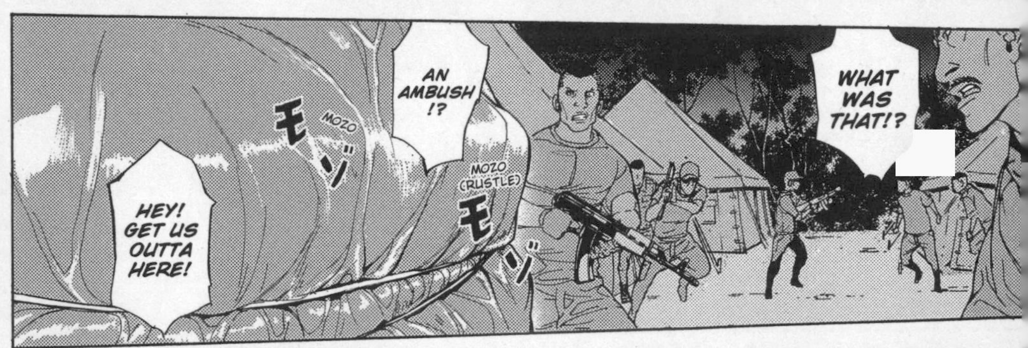
WHAT WAS THAT!?
AN AMBUSH !?
MOZO
MOZO (RUSTLE)
HEY! GET US OUTTA HERE!

!?
WHO ARE YOU!?

HYU (SWISH)

ZUGA (SHUD)
DOSU (SHUMP)
DOGA (WHAM)
BAKI (CRACK)
CHA (CLICK)
WHA—
DOSU

HYUN (SWISH)
HYUN
HYUN
DOSU (THUD)
DOSU
DOSU
DOSU
DON'T MOVE!
!?
AREN'T YOU—?

WE HAVE FULLY DISARMED YOUR CAMP.

IF YOU DO NOT COMPLY WITH OUR DEMANDS...

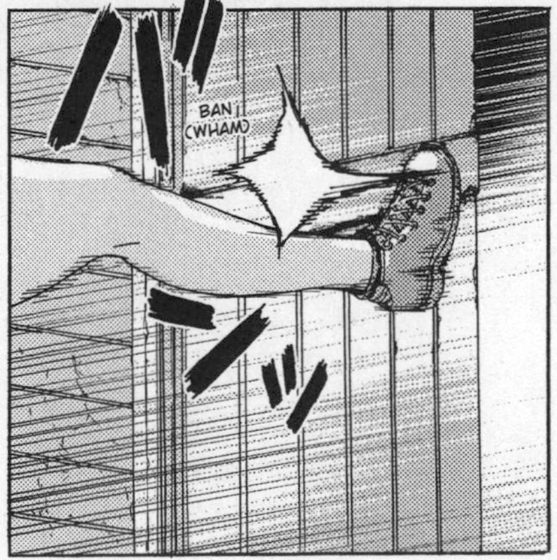
BAN
(WHAM)

ボッ
BO (WHOOM)
...WE WILL FORCE YOU TO DO SO.

...

!?

THERE ARE TWO PATROLMEN ON THE RIGHT, SENJI-SAN.

チャッ
CHA (CHK)

I HEAR AND OBEY!

Provide backup, Ashe-san.
I don't want them hurt. Miss as close as you can.
KURU (SPIN)
ROGER.

H-HEY!

HUH ...?

IS THAT —!?

YOU'RE MINE !!
ZUGA (SLICE)
GAKH!!
DOGA (THWAM)
GWAAAH!
WHUH !?
RRGH ...
WILL THAT DO, MISS?
YES!

キキッ
KIKI (SCREECH)

ガチャッ
GACHA (CLICK)

???

BUT IF WE MADE CONTACT NORMALLY, WE DETERMINED IT WOULD RESULT IN A FIREFIGHT. THEREFORE, SLIGHTLY ROUGHER MEANS WERE NECESSARY.

I'M SORRY, EVERY-ONE.

?

I APOLOGIZE FOR HAVING TO TAKE THESE MEASURES AGAINST YOU.

ARE YOU MEMBERS OF THE DUHANA LIBERATION FRONT?
ER...
YES, THAT'S US.

CAN WE ASK FOR YOUR ASSISTANCE?

???

BUOOO
(VRRRM)

Until Death do us Part

YOU EXPECT ME TO BELIEVE THIS?
YES.
AND YOU WANT US TO HELP YOU, WHEN WE HAVE NO CONNECTION TO THIS MAN?
YES.
...
...I DON'T EVEN KNOW HOW TO RESPOND ...

chapter 176

WE'RE HERE, NEXT TO THE INLAND BORDER. GOT THAT?
HERE IN THIS SWAMPY REGION, THE BORDER AND INTERIOR SECURITY...
DUHANA
...ARE MANAGED BY TAUS OF THE TURUS FAMILY. HE IS OUR DIRECT OPPONENT.
...

IN THE BARREN HIGHLANDS CLOSER TO THE CAPITAL IS GIDO.
ALONG THE SEA NEAR THE CAPITAL IS EDGE, AND FURTHER UP THE COAST IS MISALT.
THESE FOUR MEN ARE THE CLOSEST TO BEING ZASHID'S HEIR.
タウス
TAUS
DUHANA
ミサルト
MISALT
ギド
GIDO
ZOTT
エジー
EDGE
GALBOA
sea

EACH OF THEM CONTROLS ABOUT THREE TO FOUR THOUSAND MEN. THAT'S ABOUT HALF THE COUNTRY'S FORCES IN TOTAL.

THERE ARE OTHER BROTHERS IN VARIOUS ASSIGNMENTS AND LOCATIONS ...
...BUT THE MOST IMPORTANT POSTS BELONG TO GENIE AND FEN.

THE OTHERS ARE NON-COMBATANTS OR WOMEN—ESSENTIALLY NO MORE THAN CIVILIANS.

THERE ARE THAT MANY SIBLINGS?

IT MEANS THAT GENETICS EXIST TO CREATE THE STRONGEST POSSIBLE OFFSPRING.
HIS "WIFE" IS ONLY FOR PUBLIC PURPOSES. HE HAS AT LEAST THIRTY OF THEM, AND OVER A HUNDRED CHILDREN, I'VE HEARD.

THEY'RE A LINE OF MONSTERS THAT EXIST TO TEST ALL POSSIBILITIES.
SOME HAVE GREAT STRENGTH; SOME, GREAT INTELLIGENCE; SOME, SWIFT SPEED. IT IS A MIX OF MANY BLOODLINES.

THAT IS HOW ZASHID TURUS WAS CREATED.
OUR FOE IS A GREAT AND TERRIBLE MONSTER.

AND YOU STILL INTEND TO CHALLENGE HIM?

IN EXCHANGE FOR YOUR COOPERATION ...
...WE WILL OFFER TO DEFEAT TAUS OURSELVES.

...
SU (SHH)
ス

IS THIS ACCEPT-ABLE?
...VERY WELL...

BUT THERE MUST BE NO KILLING.
AFTER SEIZING HIM, HE WILL BE PUT TO A FAIR TRIAL. THAT IS MY CONDITION.
......
...
F-FINE...

"DON'T KILL HIM," SHE SAYS...
ONCE SHE SEES TAUS FOR HERSELF, SHE'LL UNDERSTAND WHAT THE SONS OF A MONSTER ARE LIKE.

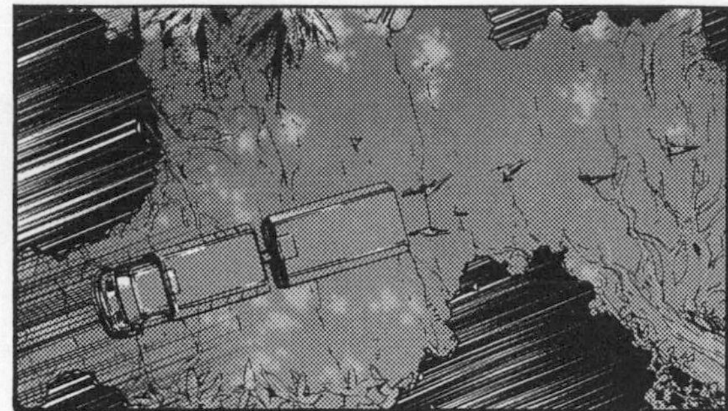

ブォォォ
BUOOO
(VRMM)

BUOO (VRMM)

BATAN (SLAM)

HAUL HIM OUT!!

DOSA (THUMP)
HRGH!

I-IS THIS—!?
THAT'S RIGHT.
GUI (TUG)
YOUR HIDDEN VILLA, RIGHT IN THE MIDST OF THE REGION YOU COMMANDED.
DOSA (THUMP)
VERY CLEVER OF YOU TO HAVE A SAFE SPACE SQUIRRELED AWAY FOR YOURSELF, EVEN IN DUHANA.

WHAT DO YOU PLAN TO ACCOMPLISH BY BRINGING ME HERE!?

YOU'RE GOING TO LEAD A REBELLION.
WHAT !?

ONE OF ZASHID TURUS'S HEIRS ESCAPES HIS EXECUTION AND BITES BACK AGAINST HIS FATHER'S HAND TO SAVE HIS OWN LIFE.
THIS WILL BE THE INITIATION OF OUR PLAN.

I-I REFUSE!
I COULD NEVER DO SOMETHING LIKE THAT TO MY DAD!!

YOUR WILL DOESN'T ENTER INTO IT.
THE WAR THAT'S ABOUT TO KICK OFF WITHIN DUHANA WILL ALL REST ON YOUR SHOULDERS.

NOW I GET IT!
THIS IS WHY YOU DIDN'T WANT ME TO BE ARRESTED IN JAPAN, ISN'T IT!?

YEP! YOU HAVE TO GO MISSING, OR ELSE YOU'VE GOT AN ALIBI.

!?

YOU SADISTIC...
HOW ...
HOW MUCH MUST I SUFFER ...
... BEFORE YOU ARE SATISFIED?

HOW ABOUT ...
...UNTIL YOU REGRET THAT YOU WERE EVER BORN?

FUC—

CHA (CHK)

......
THIS IS NO JOKE. I AM DEADLY SERIOUS.
THIS IS THE RESULT OF YOUR ACTIONS THAT DAMAGED THE LIFE OF A YOUNG GIRL!

YOU REAP WHAT YOU SOW.
THE KARMA OF YOUR SINS COMES BACK AROUND TO REVISIT YOU. HAPPENS ALL THE TIME.

...WH-WHO DO YOU THINK YOU ARE NOW... GOD?

I'LL REPEAT—YOU ARE THE ONE WHO TOYED WITH HARUKA'S FATE.

DID YOU THINK THAT JUST BECAUSE YOU'RE THE SON OF A TYRANT THAT RUINING THE LIVES OF OTHERS WOULD NEVER COME BACK TO AFFECT YOU?
FUCK ME? FUCK YOU!
...

NEXT.

WHAT, THERE'S MORE!?

OF COURSE THERE'S MORE. YOU'RE STILL ALIVE, AREN'T YOU!?

...

LET'S SEE...
THAT'S THE CAMERAS AND THE EDITING EQUIPMENT.
ドサッ
DOSA (THUMP)

IT FIGURES THAT THIS PLACE'S INTERNET FUNCTIONALITY IS UTTER SHIT...

IT'S ALMOST CRUEL IN ITS RUTHLESS-NESS...

BUT EDGE HAS TOO MUCH PRIDE TO CHOOSE DEATH FOR HIMSELF.
KNOWING THIS, THE PLAN IS TO PUSH HIM AS FAR AS HE'LL GO.

AREN'T YOU HIS FORMER MENTOR?
THIS HAPPENED TO HIM BECAUSE HE DABBLED IN SADISTIC CRUELTY FOR FUN.

I CERTAINLY DIDN'T TEACH HIM THAT QUALITY.
CRIME OUGHT TO BE SMART AND EFFICIENT.
IF MY METHODS APPEARED RUTHLESS AS A RESULT, WELL, I CAN'T HELP THAT, ZELM.

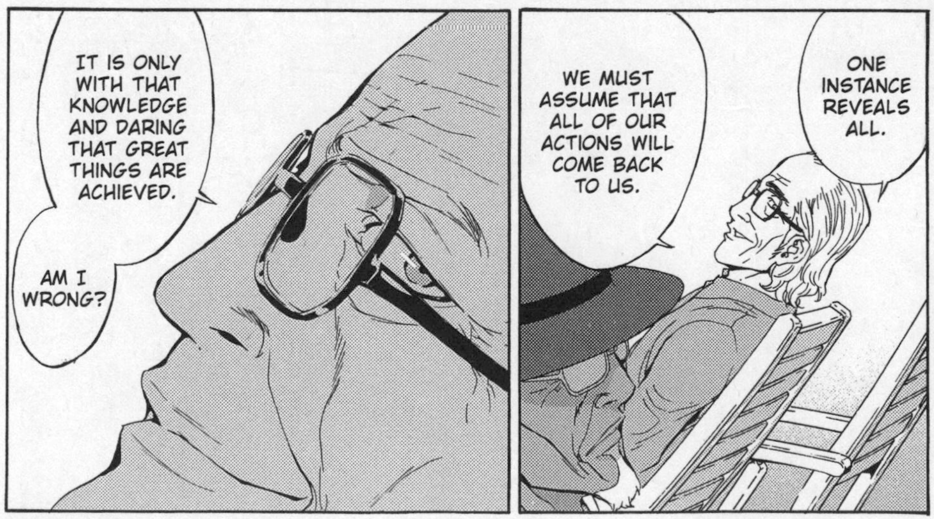
ONE INSTANCE REVEALS ALL.
WE MUST ASSUME THAT ALL OF OUR ACTIONS WILL COME BACK TO US.
IT IS ONLY WITH THAT KNOWLEDGE AND DARING THAT GREAT THINGS ARE ACHIEVED.
AM I WRONG?

...

BUT I DON'T THINK SPOILED LITTLE EDGE WILL EVER UNDERSTAND THAT.

AS ANOTHER FORMER PUPIL, IT HURTS TO WATCH.

YA KNOW?

ドッン
DOON (BOOM)
ドガァ
DOGAA (KABOOM)

The bombing of this base was carried out...
...by me—Edge Turus, son of Zashid Turus.

In order to return power from the corrupt regime to the people and my father.
As of today, I declare war as his rightful heir.
This is not rebellion. I am fighting to reclaim my father's power from Galboa.

WELL CONSTRUCTED, THAT RECORDING... AND YOU BROADCAST IT RIGHT IN THE PROPER RADIO WAVELENGTHS.
IT WASN'T TOO HARD.
HE REALLY DIDN'T WANT TO SAY THE MESSAGE PROPERLY, SO I HAD TO DO SOME EDITING...
THINK THEY'LL NOTICE?

THIS KIND OF TRICKERY WON'T SUCCEED IN ROUSTING ZASHID, BUT IT'S ALL WE NEED FOR NOW.

WE'RE PRODDING THE WEAK POINT OF A DICTATORIAL REGIME.
WEAK POINT?

THAT'S RIGHT. WE'RE GOING TO STRANGLE THEM WITH SILK.

Until Death do us Part

chapter 177

EDGE TURUS, LEADING A REBELLION?

HE'D NEVER DO SUCH A THING, WOULD HE?

EXACTLY!
SO WHAT IS THAT BROADCAST SUPPOSED TO MEAN!?
DUNNO...

THERE'S NO WAY ZASHID TURUS WOULD BE SHAKEN BY MUTINY FROM HIM.
BUT GIVEN THAT IT'S WISEMAN WHO'S PULLING THE STRINGS FROM THE SHADOWS...
...I CAN'T IMAGINE THAT CAUSING CONFUSION IS HIS ONLY GOAL.

MAMORU-SAN...

YOU KNOW...
WHAT'S UP?

I HATE TO SAY IT, BUT THESE GUYS ARE INCREDIBLY UNDER-FUNDED.

WEAK WEAPONS, OLD VEHICLES, AND LOW NUMBERS—THOUGH I KNOW THIS ISN'T THEIR FULL FORCE.
AND GUERRILLA WARFARE IS GALBOA'S SPECIALTY.
THAT'S HOW THEY GAINED THEIR INDEPENDENCE. OBVIOUSLY THE OFFICIAL ARMY HAS THE ADVANTAGE.

THEY'RE NOT EVEN FIT TO CALL THEMSELVES THE "LIBERATION FRONT."
...

...
INDEED. OVER EIGHTY PERCENT OF THE COUNTRY'S MIGHT IS ALLIED WITH ZASHID.
MOST OF THE OPPOSING NUMBER GETS FORCED OUT OF THE COUNTRY—LIKE ME.

IT'S VALUABLE TO HAVE ANY SORT OF RESISTANCE WITHIN THE BORDER, IF YOU ASK ME.

PLEASE OFFER ME REAL TIME INTERPRE-TATION.
Yes, Miss Haruka.

AS ORDERED, WE'LL SURROUND THEM, ATTACK, THEN BACK OFF AT ONCE.
THE REST WILL BE UP TO YOUR TEAM.

YOU'RE SURE YOU WANT TO START THIS?

YES. ACCORDING TO OUR DATA, TAUS TURUS IS A CLASSIC, IMPULSIVE WARRIOR.
WE WILL CONFRONT HIM DIRECTLY AND DEFEAT HIM, PROVING OUR SUPERIORITY.

To our advantage, this area is quite swampy ...

...which makes heavy combat vehicles useless.

Plus, the enemy is comfortable with guerrilla warfare, and I predict they will not mobilize a large force against so few.

In particular, Taus Turus is known to be highly confident and a candidate for most powerful in battle among the brothers.

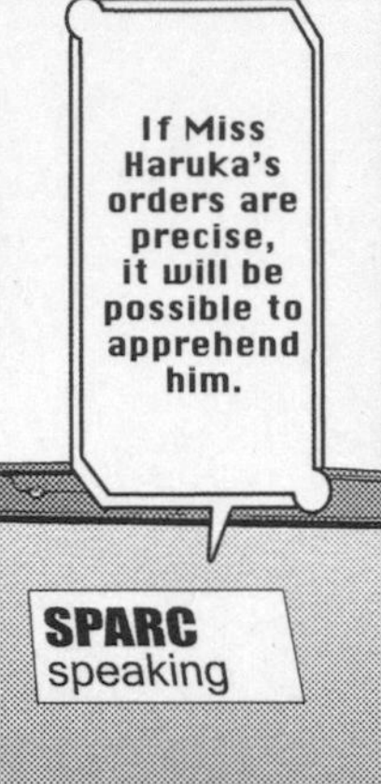
If Miss Haruka's orders are precise, it will be possible to apprehend him.
SPARC speaking

IN EITHER CASE, THE RESULT WILL DEPEND ON ME, THEN.
Yes, Miss Haruka.

This is a terrain map of the area, based on satellite photography.

ANA
Reports say the advance party's preparations are proceeding smoothly.
From that point of view...
...I would be against even sending you there.
BUT CAN I REALLY BE A LEADER...?
SHOULDN'T YOU BE GIVING THE COMMANDS?
I under-stand your concern.
However, as I am programmed to prioritize human life, I cannot give dangerous orders.
...

If you simply cannot make the hard decision, lean upon your squad members.
We have chosen them for that purpose.
As Shot has the least familiarity with you, he is the most likely to be fair-minded.
...I UNDERSTAND.
However!
WHAT?
I would remove him from consideration where the locals are concerned.
BUOOO (VRMMM)
TA (-TAT-) TA TA TA

LET'S GO, EVERY-ONE!
ROGER.
ガチャ
GACHA (CLICK)
TRANSFER-RING DRIVE CONTROL TO SPARC.

WHAT WE'RE ABOUT TO FACE NOW IS JUST THE FIRST WAVE!
WE MUST DISARM THEM QUICKLY TO GET THE MAIN FORCE ACTIVE.

...SHIT...
WHEN'S MY TURN...?

TA (TAT) TA TA
TA TA TA
TA TA TA TA

DA (DASH) DA DA
GACHA (CHUNK)
CHA (CLICK)
UUU (WOOOO)

BA (BRUMM)
B
BA
BA
BA

ASHE-SAN!

I'M ON IT.

SLOW SPEED. SWITCH SNIPING POINT TO TOOYAMA'S ORDERS.

Yes, Miss Ashe.

A MOVING SNIPER'S A GOOD TACTIC...
...BUT THE ORDER'S ON THE DIFFICULT SIDE.

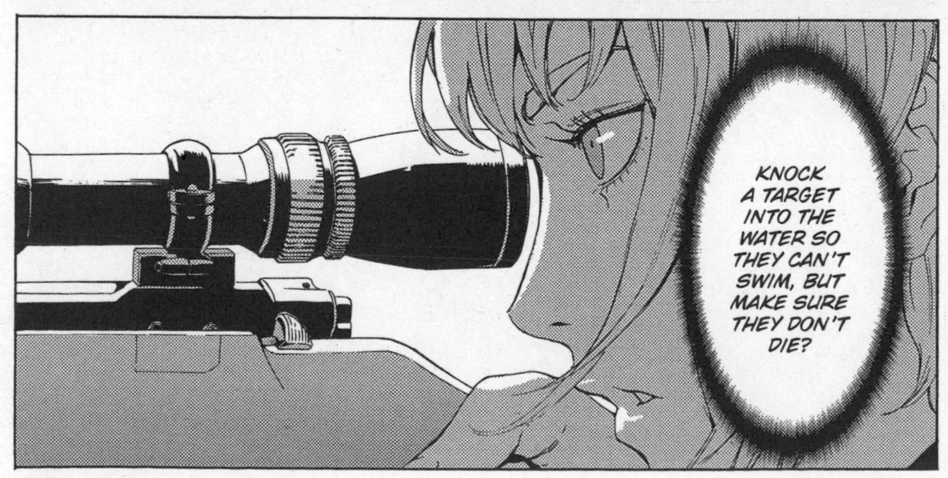
KNOCK A TARGET INTO THE WATER SO THEY CAN'T SWIM, BUT MAKE SURE THEY DON'T DIE?

BASHU
(BZOOM)
KAKIN
(KCHING)
BASHU
GASHA
(SHUNK)
GUESS I SHOULD THANK HER PLACEMENT.

タタタタタ
TA
TA
TA
TA

タタタタタタ
TA
TA
TA
TA
TA
TA

タタタタタ
TA
TA
TA
TA
TA

NICE. ALMOST THERE.

NOW!
KACHI (CLICK)
カチッ

BOSHU (BZOOM)
ボシュッ
!!?
BURA (LURCH)
ブラッ
!?
ZUBU (FWUNK)
ズブ
ZUBU
ズブ

WHAT THE —!?
DOSHAAA (SHWUBB)

DON (BOOM)
DON
DON
IT'S CALLED A "LIQUEFACTION EXPLOSION"!

SMAK!
....

BYU
(ZWIP)
KIN
(TING)
KA
(WHAK)
KA
BYU

BAKI (CRACK)
BA (WHOOSH)
GA (WHAM)
KAN (TAK)
DOSU (THUD)
KYUN (ZWING)

WE'VE NEUTRAL-IZED THE LEAD PARTY, EVERYONE.
Find safe cover for now.
Here he comes!

ZA (MARCH)
ZA
ZA

Don't bother shooting him.
HE'S... HUGE!

THE ONLY ONE WHO CAN BEAT HIM WITHOUT KILLING HIM...
BUSHUU (FSSH)
system check
ENGINE START
N
0km/h
...is Ibuki-san.

ZA (SCREEE)
ZA
ZA
I NEARLY DIED WAITING!!

chapter 178

WHERE DID YOU SEND THE BLACK UNIT!?

...

WHERE ARE THEY CARRYING OUT YOUR PLAN!?

WOULD YOU MIND NOT INTERRUPTING MY VALUABLE READING TIME, FORMER DIPLOMAT TURUS?

I AM NOT SOFT ENOUGH TO GIVE YOU UNNECESSARY INFORMATION OUT OF SYMPATHY.

WHAT ARE YOU PLOTTING!? WHAT AM I BEING USED TO DO!?
DO YOU REALLY THINK THIS IS GOING TO UNNERVE MY DAD, OF ALL PEOPLE!?

BUSHU (DSHT)

AAGH!!

SILENCE!

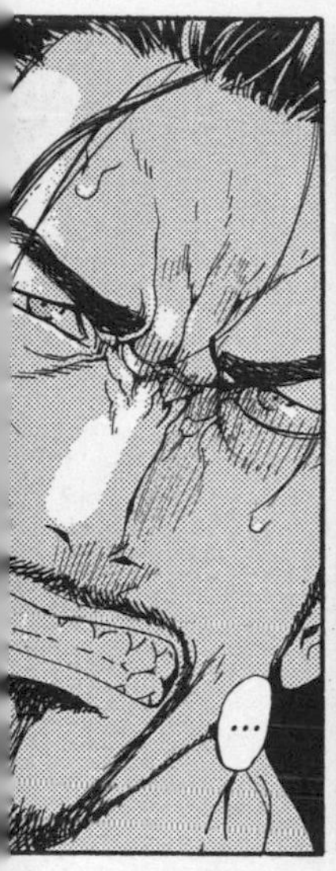
...

ガチャッ
GACHA (CLICK)
TIME'S UP.
THANK GOD.
I CAN FINALLY READ IN PEACE.

IF HE'S THAT MUCH OF A BOTHER, JUST KILL HIM.

BURY HIM IN THE JUNGLE OUT BACK AND NOBODY WILL FIND HIM FOR A WHILE.
FREES UP A PAIR OF EYES FROM GUARD DUTY TOO.

IF HE MAKES TOO MUCH NOISE, YOU'RE FREE TO CARRY OUT THAT OPTION.
...
...

BUT DEPENDING ON THE CIRCUM-STANCES, HE MIGHT STILL HOLD SOME USE...

BUN
BUN (WHOOSH)
HYU (SWISH)

タ
TA (TAT)
タ
TA
タ
TA
タ
TA
カーン
GAN (CLANK)
ガッ
GA
ガッ
GA (BLAM)
タ
TA
タ
TA
タ
TA

THE ELECTRIC MOTORCYCLE BUCEPHALUS, THE HIGH-WATER MARK OF VEHICLE TECHNOLOGY, HAS ONE MAJOR WEAKNESS—SHORT OPERATION TIME.

DAI-SAN, THE ENEMY LEADER IS MOVING TO THE PREDICTED LOCATION.
GOT-CHA!

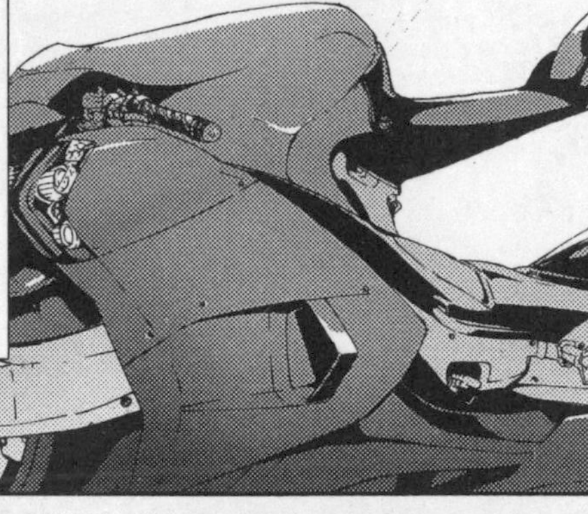
IT WAS USED IN FIGHTING SERIOUS URBAN CRIME DESPITE THIS FLAW BECAUSE OF ITS UNPARALLELED EFFECTIVE-NESS.
EVEN WITH EXTRA-LARGE CAPACITY BATTERIES AND FUEL CELLS, ITS OPERATION TIME IS NO MORE THAN TWENTY MINUTES AT MAX OUTPUT.
IF THE POWER CONSUMPTION IS HELD UNDER THE RECHARGE RATE, THAT NUMBER COULD BE LENGTHENED, BUT THE DIFFERENCE WOULD BE TINY IN THE SPAN OF THIS BATTLE.

THE CRUX OF THIS OPERATION LIES IN HOW WELL THIS TOOL IS UTI-LIZED.
GOTTA KNOCK OUT TAUS AND HIS DIRECT TROOPS ALL AT ONCE!

GET A LOAD OF THIS, NEW GUYS!!

DID THEY REALLY NEUTRALIZE THE ENTIRE ADVANCE UNIT?

BUT... THE REAL PROBLEM IS THE MAIN FORCE AFTER THEM...

BA (VRRM)
BA
BA
BA

TA (TAT)
TA
TA
TA

PII (BEEP)
PII
PII
PII
PII

BYU
SHOOT ALL!
BYU (BAM)
WHRP!
BIRI
BIRI (BZZT)
BIRI
BIRI
1
2
3
4
5
DOSA (THUMP)
DOSA

ドッ
DOGA (WHUD)
ガッ
ビリ
BIRI
ビリ
BIRI
ビリ
BIRI
URGH!
AAH!
GAAAH!

バッ
BA (ZOOM)

タ
TA
(TAT)
タ
TA
タ
TA
タ
TA
タ
TA
タ
TA
タ
TA
タ
TA
ビリ
BIRI
(BZZAP)
SHOOT ALL!
ビリ
BIRI
バシャ
BASHA
(SMACK)
ビリ
BIRI
ビリ
BIRI

WHAT IS THIS... WATER?!
DAMN! IS HE IN FULLY-INSULATED ARMOR!?
GASHI (KCHK)
!?
DO (BLAM)
DO
DO
KIKI (SCREECH)
DO
DO

DO (BLAM)
DO
DO
DO
DO
IT MOVES LIKE A FREAK...
HOW STRONG IS THIS GUY!?
DO
DO
DO
DO
DO

HYUUN
(ZWOOM)
KAN
(TANG)
KAKAN
UGH!!
GA
(WHAK)

SPARC SPEAKING
Overusing the stun shot raises the danger of running out of power.
GYUN (ZOOM)
I GET IT, I GET IT!!
WHAT!?
WHA—!?
BABABA (BRRRM)
ATA (SPLAT)
TA
GAN (WHANK)
GA (WHAM)
HYUN (SWISH)
KAN (CLANG)

ZUGAGAGA (ZDOOM)
BAGI (KCHUNK)
GASHI (FUMP)
DOGA (THUD)
WELL? DID THAT SAVE ENOUGH POWER FOR YA!?
Yes, Dai.

CHA
(SHK)
チャ…

WHAT DO YOU SAY, BOSS? ONE-ON-ONE?
OR ARE YOU TOO BIG OF A PUSSY!?

...
SO I SUPPOSE THIS GUN IS WORTHLESS...

...AGAINST SIMILAR ARMOR AS MINE...
GASHA
(CHUNK)
ガシャッ

ZU...
(ZMMF)
ズ
...

I WILL DESTROY YOU NOW.

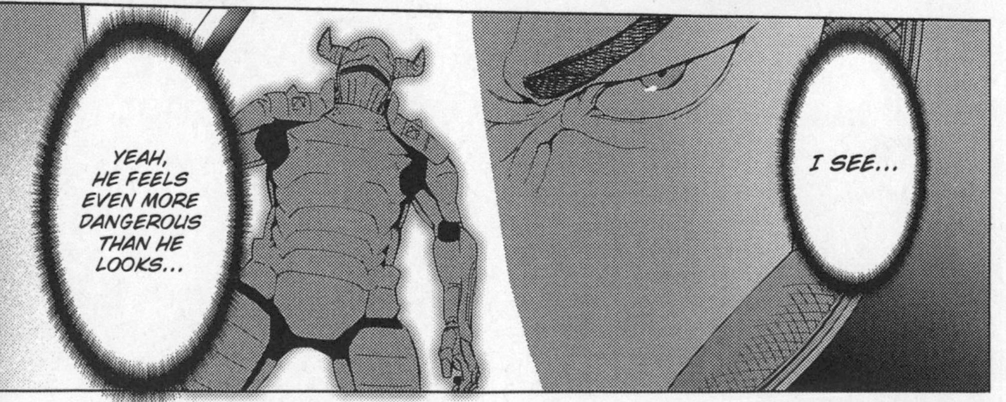
I SEE...
YEAH, HE FEELS EVEN MORE DANGEROUS THAN HE LOOKS...

ELAN-SAN, SHOT-SAN, KEEP THE TROOPS AWAY FROM DAI-SAN!
ROGER.
HIS BATTERY LEVELS ARE BELOW HALF.
ROGER.

...
HYUO (SWOOSH)
BUO (VOOM)
PERO (LICK)

BA
(WOOSH)
DOGO
(CRUNCH)

BUT NOT EVEN HIGH-CALIBER ROUNDS CAN PIERCE THIS SPECIAL ARMOR!!
GA (WHAM)

キュ
KYURURURU (SKREEEE)
RAAAAAAAAAAA
AAAAAH!!!
HE TOOK A BODY SHOT FROM 660 POUNDS OF BUCEPHALUS!
ピー
PII (BEEP)
ピー
PII
ピー
PII
ピー
PII
ピー
PII
ピー
PII

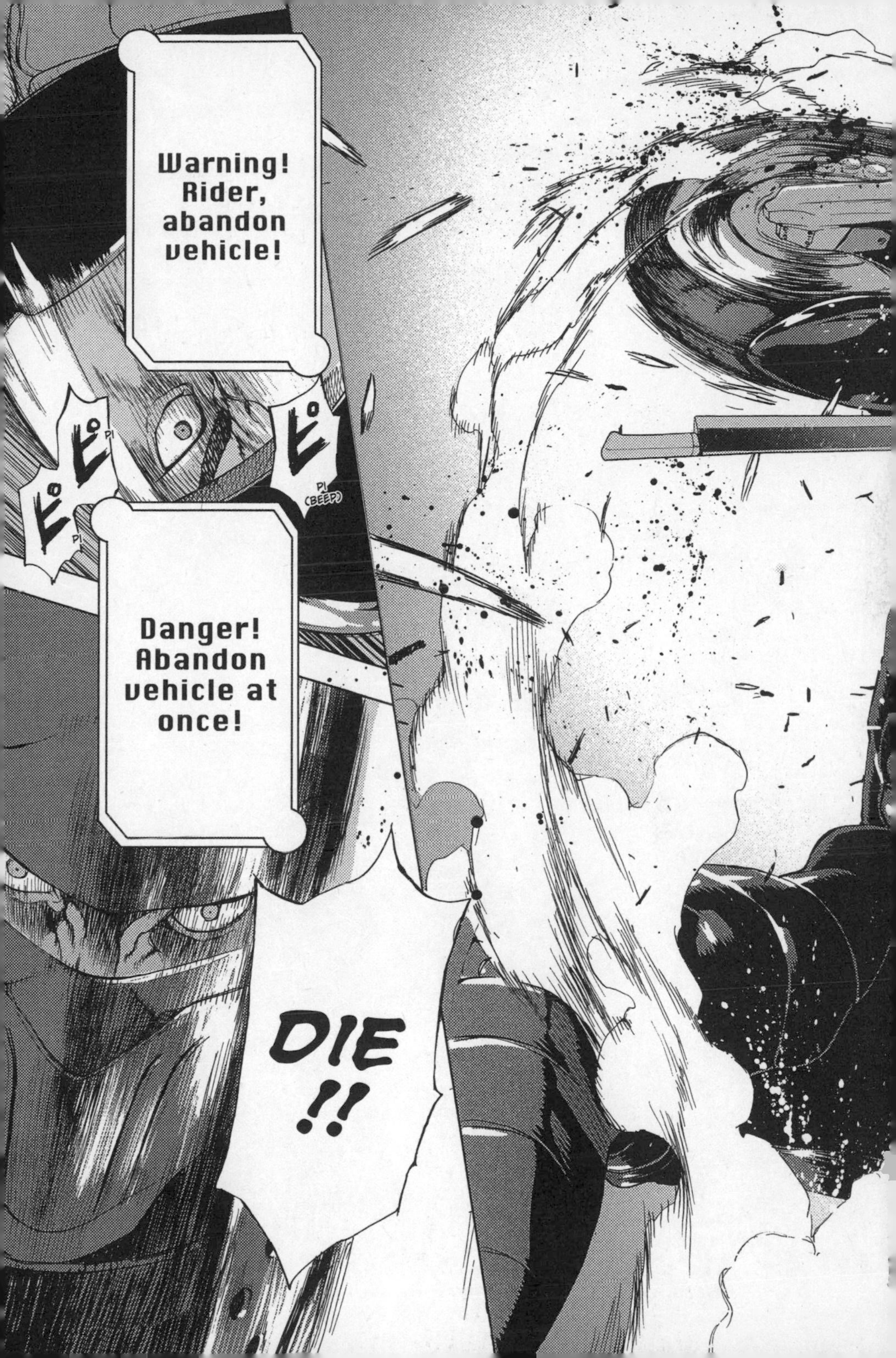

Warning! Rider, abandon vehicle!
ピ
PI (BEEP)
ピ PI
ピ PI
ピ PI
Danger! Abandon vehicle at once!
DIE!!

until death do us part ⑪ – end

BA
(ZOOM)

POLICE CAT
CATHERINE

警察猫
POLICE CAT
社団
法人
NIPPON POLICE
KYAO!
POLICE

A NEW WEAPON

ORGANIZED CRIME ONLY GETS WORSE BY THE DAY.

EVEN POLICE DOGS ARE HELPLESS TO STOP THE RISING TIDE...

FINALLY, THE AUTHORITIES UNVEIL A NEW WEAPON TO FIGHT CRIME!

THE POLICE CAT!
NICE TO MEOWT YOU.
POLICE
SO CUTE.
SO CUTE.

ON THE CHASE

ENCOUNTER

Art Staff
Suri ♀: Chief Assistant
0-Second ♂: Background Art
Taurus ♀: Background Art

Military Advisor
Lee Hyun Seok (warmania)

SPECIAL THANKS
Shingo Takano

Crossover Planning
JESUS—Sajin Kouro, Yami no Aegis, Akatsuki no Aegis
Written by Kyouichi Nanatsuki, Art by Yoshihide Fujiwara
(Shogakukan)

Design Assistance
Hitoshi Fukuchi

Until Death do us Part

Translation Notes

Common Honorifics
no honorific: Indicates familiarity or closeness; if used without permission or reason, addressing someone in this manner would constitute an insult.
***-san*:** The Japanese equivalent of Mr./Mrs./Miss. If a situation calls for politeness, this is the fail-safe honorific.
***-sama*:** Conveys great respect; may also indicate that the social status of the speaker is lower than that of the addressee.
***-kun*:** Used most often when referring to boys, this indicates affection or familiarity. Occasionally used by older men among their peers, but it may also be used by anyone referring to a person of lower standing.
***-chan*:** An affectionate honorific indicating familiarity used mostly in reference to girls; also used in reference to cute persons or animals of either gender.
***-senpai*:** A suffix used to address upperclassmen or more experienced coworkers.
***-sensei*:** A respectful term for teachers, artists, or high-level professionals.

Yen conversion: While exchange rates fluctuate daily, a convenient conversion estimation is about ¥100 to 1 USD.

Page 21
Tarou Urashima: A fairy tale figure who saved a turtle from some cruel children, and was taken to the underwater Dragon Palace in thanks. As he left, Urashima was given a special treasure chest called a Tamatebako, but instructed never to open it. Despite being gone only three days, he finds that he has actually been away for 300 years, and everyone he knew is now dead. When he opens the tamatebako, inside is his old age, and he is instantly aged and decrepit. In figurative terms, this name can therefore be applied to anyone who disappears and only comes back many, many years later—a Western analogue would be Rip Van Winkle.

Page 109
Naginata: A polearm that consisted of a curved katana blade on the end of a long wooden pole. The closest European equivalent would be a glaive.

Page 110
Shinai: The softer, bamboo-made sword used in modern kendo. The "blade" is made of multiple flexible bamboo slats that give somewhat when a target is struck, making them much safer to use.

Page 135
Danzai: The Japanese word for "conviction" or "condemnation."

Page 199
Donichi: This character's name, Eiichi, is written with the kanji for "sharp" and "one." He had previously made a joke about being "*donichi*," or "dull one."

Page 228
Calpis: A non-carbonated beverage that contains lactic acid, giving it a bit of a yogurt-y taste. There are a number of fruit flavors of Calpis.

PAGE 235

Hagakure: A book written by Yamamoto Tsunetomo in the early 18th century, often subtitled *The Way of the Samurai* in translation, detailing Yamamoto's views on the samurai code known as "bushido." It was written after the Tokugawa shogunate had unified Japan and the fierce fighting of the Sengoku (Warring States) Era had passed, and was therefore intended to be a manual to a mindset and way of life that was, in the author's view, in danger of being lost. The title *Hagakure* means "hidden in the leaves."

Featured
Browse Store
New Releases
Fun Stuff
Library
Featured
Fun Stuff
Read all your favorite manga titles on your iPad or iPhone!

Yen Press

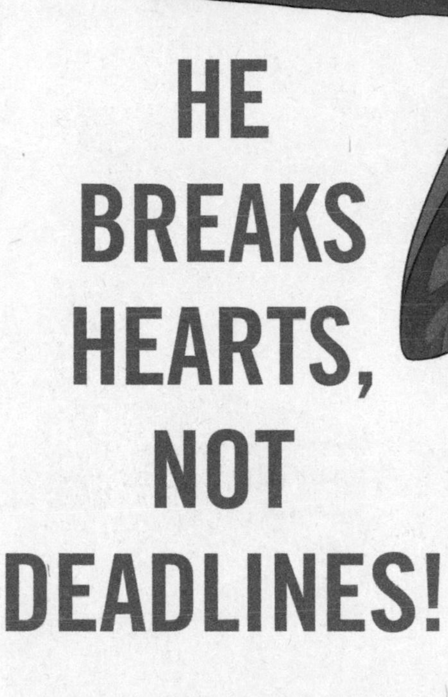

OLDER TEEN
OT
Yen Press

UNTIL DEATH DO US PART 11

HIROSHI TAKASHIGE
DOUBLE-S

Translation: Stephen Paul
Lettering: AndWorld Design

Yen Press
Hachette Book Group
1290 Avenue of the Americas
New York, NY 10104

HachetteBookGroup.com
YenPress.com

Yen Press is an imprint of Hachette Book Group, Inc. The Yen Press name and logo are trademarks of Hachette Book Group, Inc.

Library of Congress Control Number: 2015952596

First Yen Press Edition: January 2016

ISBN: 978-0-316-34023-6

10 9 8 7 6 5 4 3 2 1

BVG

Printed in the United States of America

THE POWER TO RULE THE HIDDEN WORLD OF SHINOBI...
THE POWER COVETED BY EVERY NINJA CLAN...
...LIES WITHIN THE MOST APATHETIC, DISINTERESTED VESSEL IMAGINABLE.
Nabari No Ou
Yuhki Kamatani
COMPLETE SERIES NOW AVAILABLE
OLDER TEEN OT
Yen Press
Nabari No Ou © Yuhki Kamatani / SQUARE ENIX

COLONEL.

THE REPRESENTATIVE OF THE TRANSPLANT CONNECTION IS REQUESTING TO SEE YOU AT ONCE.

KEEP HIM WAITING.

ズシャアア
ZUSHAA
(ZSSHH)

Until Death do us Part